D0180354

OUR WRETCHED TOWN HALL

TORONTO, CANADA
JANUARY,—SEPTEMBER 2018

© 2018 ERIC KOSTIUK WILLIAMS
ISBN 978-1-940398-82-2

RETROFIT 78

NO PART OF THIS BOOK MAY BE REPRODUCED
WITHOUT PERMISSION OF THE ARTIST
EXCEPT SMALL PORTIONS FOR THE PURPOSES
OF REVIEW.

PUBLISHED BY RETROFIT COMICS
AND BIG PLANET COMICS

WASHINGTON, DC
RETROFITCOMICS.COM
BIGPLANETCOMICS.COM

DISTRIBUTED BY SCB DISTRIBUTORS
PRINTED IN CANADA

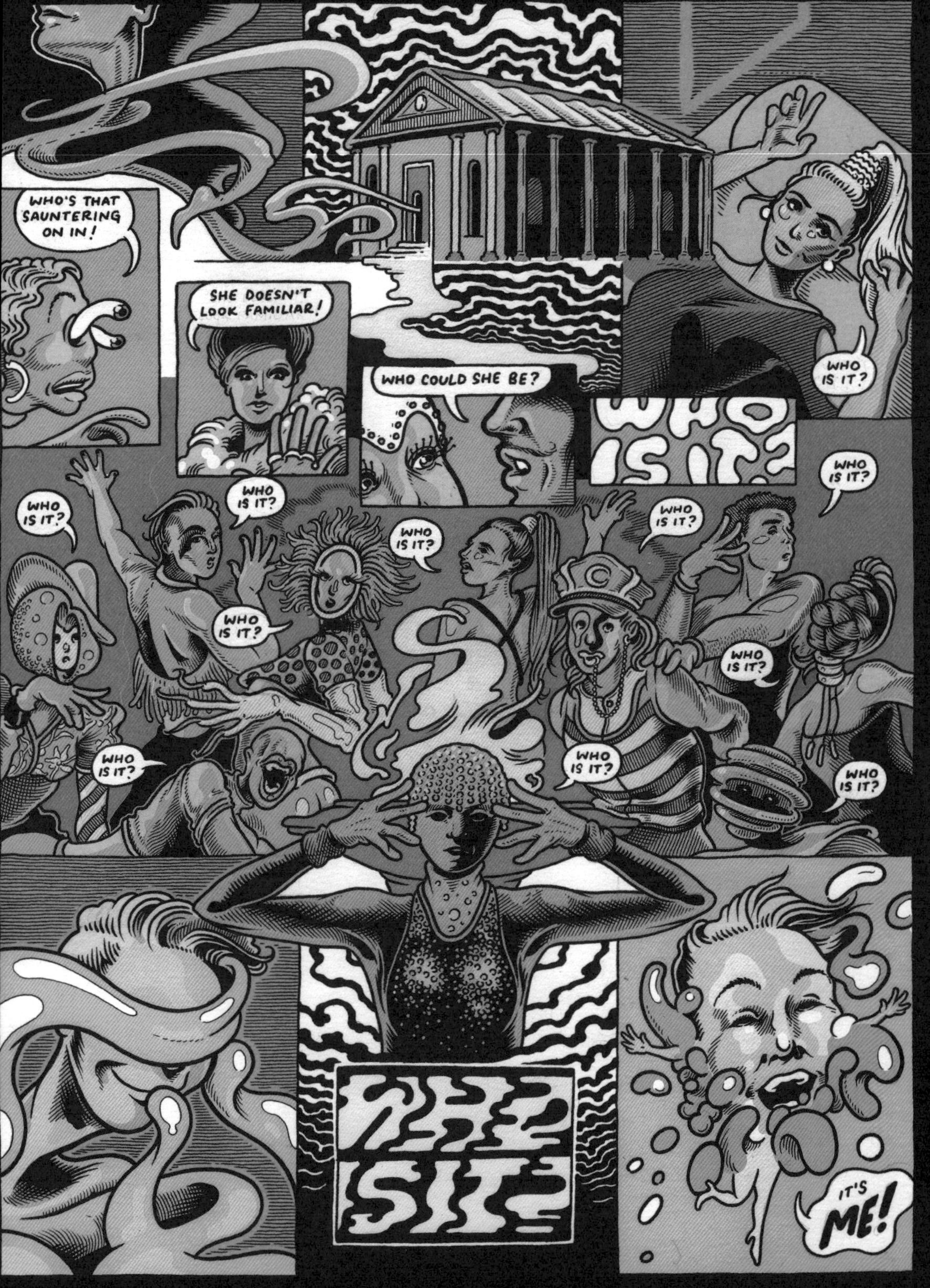
WHO'S THAT SAUNTERING ON IN!
SHE DOESN'T LOOK FAMILIAR!
WHO COULD SHE BE?
WHO IS IT?
WHO IS IT?
WHO IS IT?
WHO IS IT?
WHO IS IT?
WHO IS IT?
WHO IS IT?
WHO IS IT?
WHO IS IT?
WHO IS IT?
WHO IS IT?
WHO IS IT?
IT'S ME!

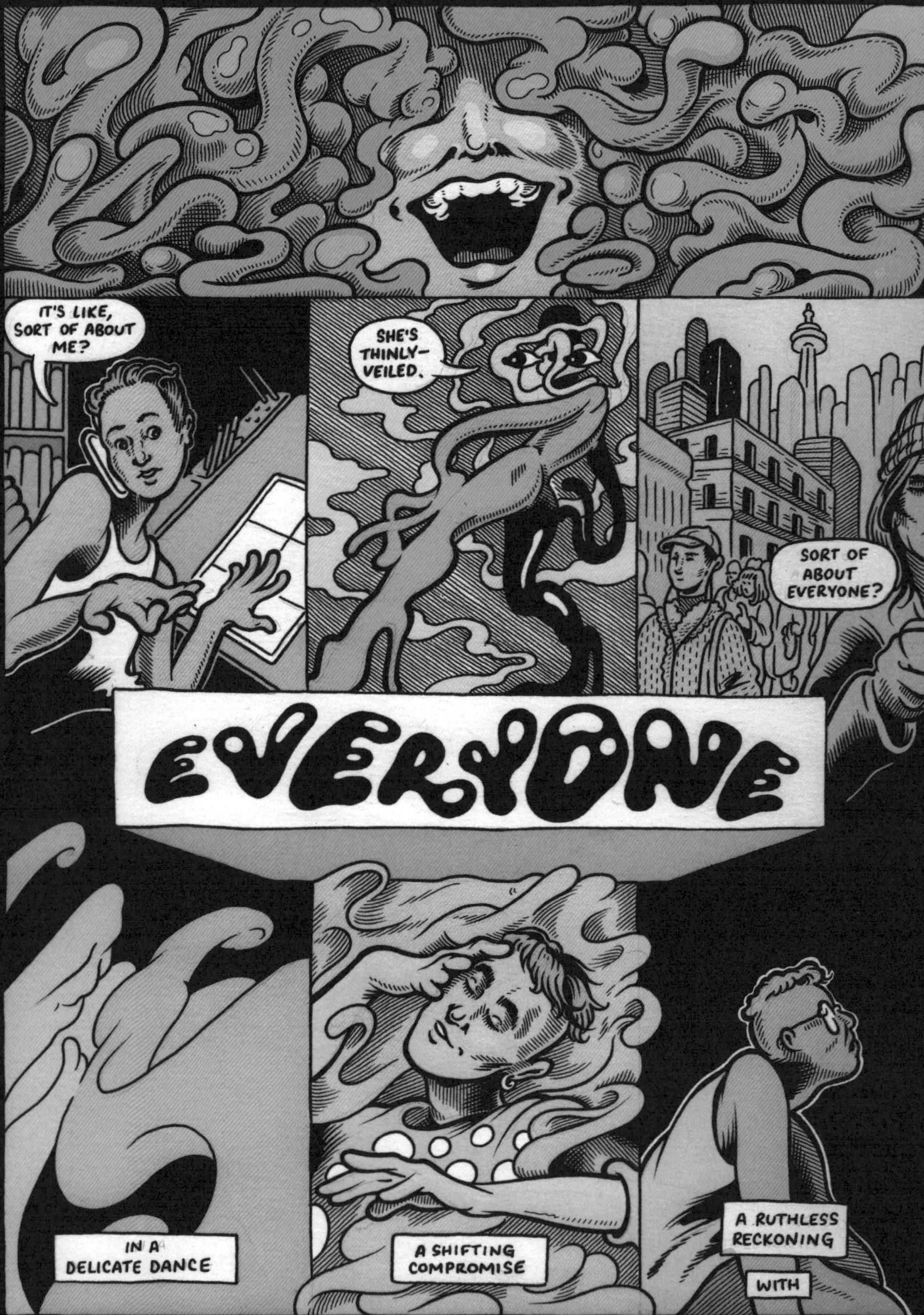
IT'S LIKE, SORT OF ABOUT ME?
SHE'S THINLY-VEILED.
SORT OF ABOUT EVERYONE?
EVERYONE
IN A DELICATE DANCE
A SHIFTING COMPROMISE
A RUTHLESS RECKONING
WITH

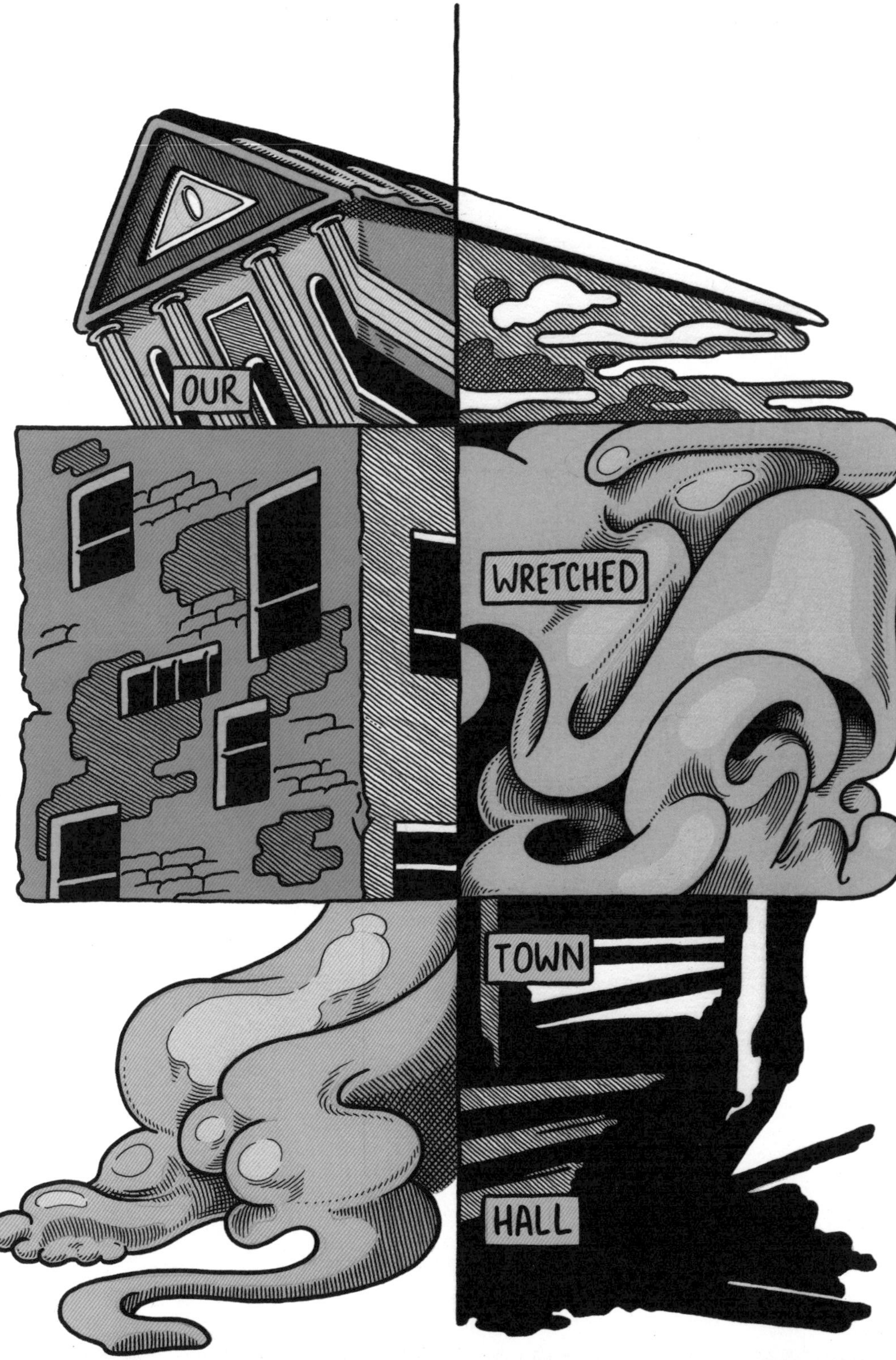
OUR
WRETCHED
TOWN
HALL

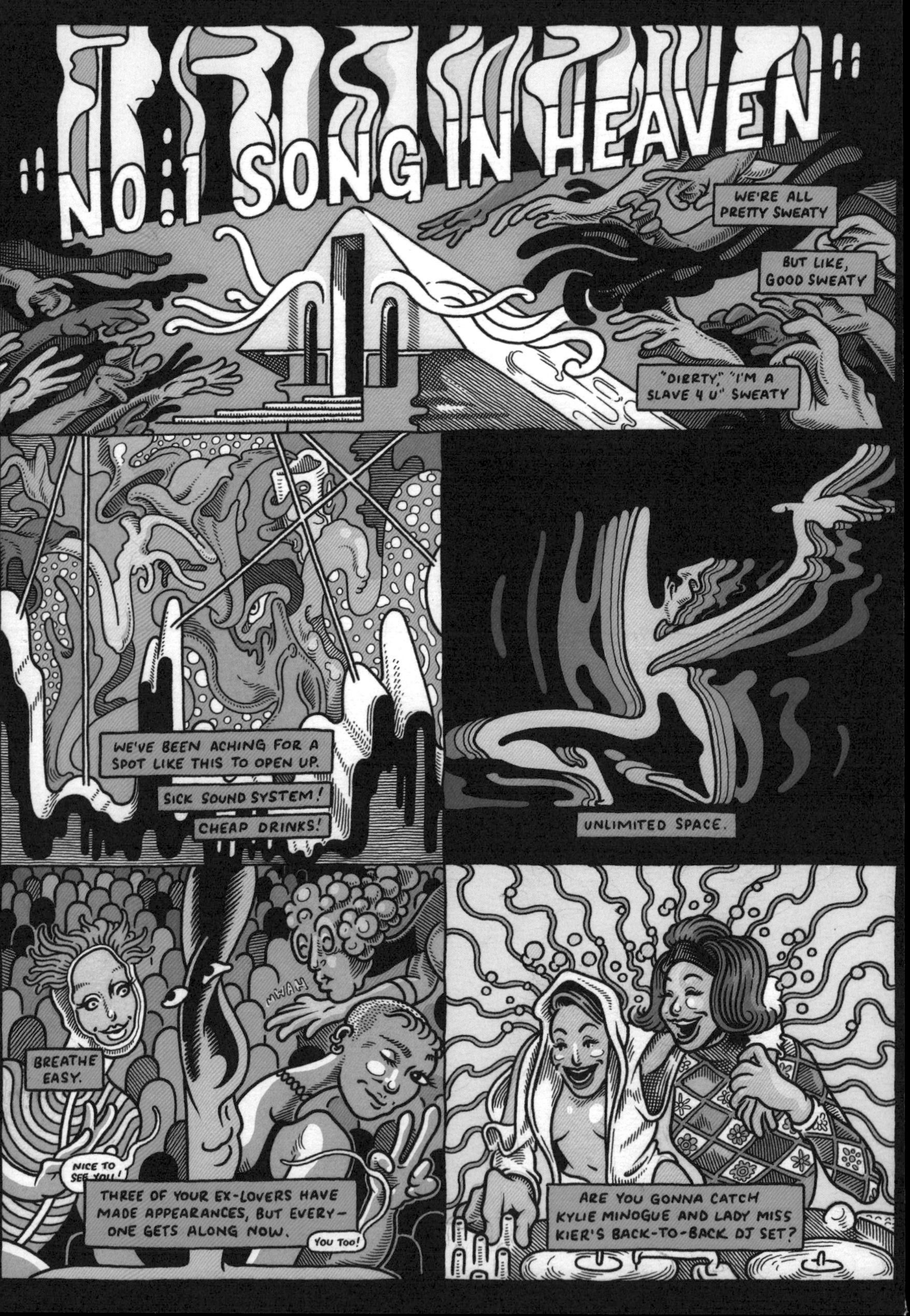
"NO. 1 SONG IN HEAVEN"
WE'RE ALL PRETTY SWEATY
BUT LIKE, GOOD SWEATY
"DIRRTY," "I'M A SLAVE 4 U" SWEATY
WE'VE BEEN ACHING FOR A SPOT LIKE THIS TO OPEN UP.
SICK SOUND SYSTEM!
CHEAP DRINKS!
UNLIMITED SPACE.
BREATHE EASY.
MWAH
NICE TO SEE YOU!
THREE OF YOUR EX-LOVERS HAVE MADE APPEARANCES, BUT EVERY-ONE GETS ALONG NOW.
YOU TOO!
ARE YOU GONNA CATCH KYLIE MINOGUE AND LADY MISS KIER'S BACK-TO-BACK DJ SET?

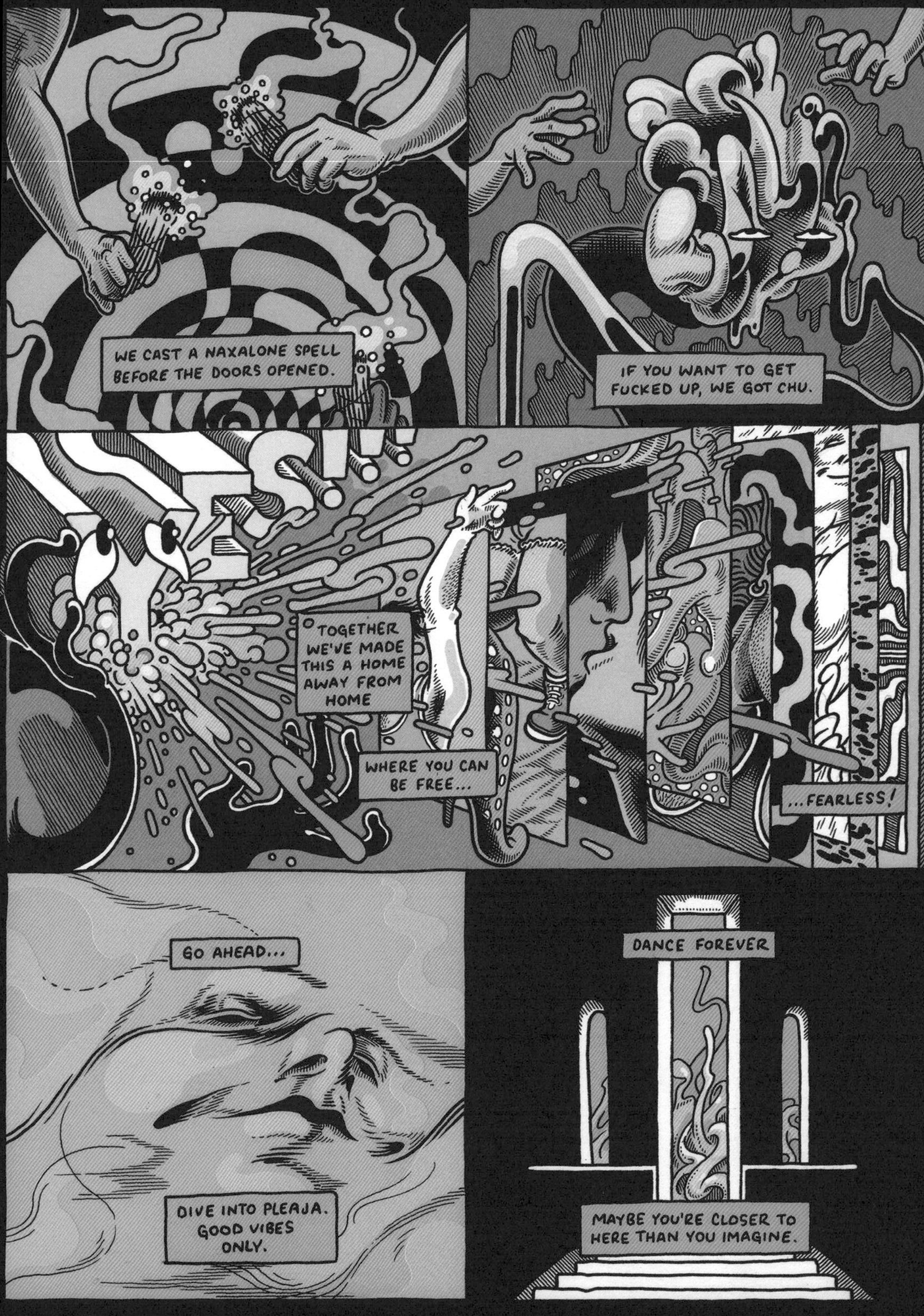
WE CAST A NAXALONE SPELL BEFORE THE DOORS OPENED.
IF YOU WANT TO GET FUCKED UP, WE GOT CHU.
TOGETHER WE'VE MADE THIS A HOME AWAY FROM HOME
WHERE YOU CAN BE FREE...
...FEARLESS!
GO AHEAD...
DIVE INTO PLEAJA. GOOD VIBES ONLY.
DANCE FOREVER
MAYBE YOU'RE CLOSER TO HERE THAN YOU IMAGINE.

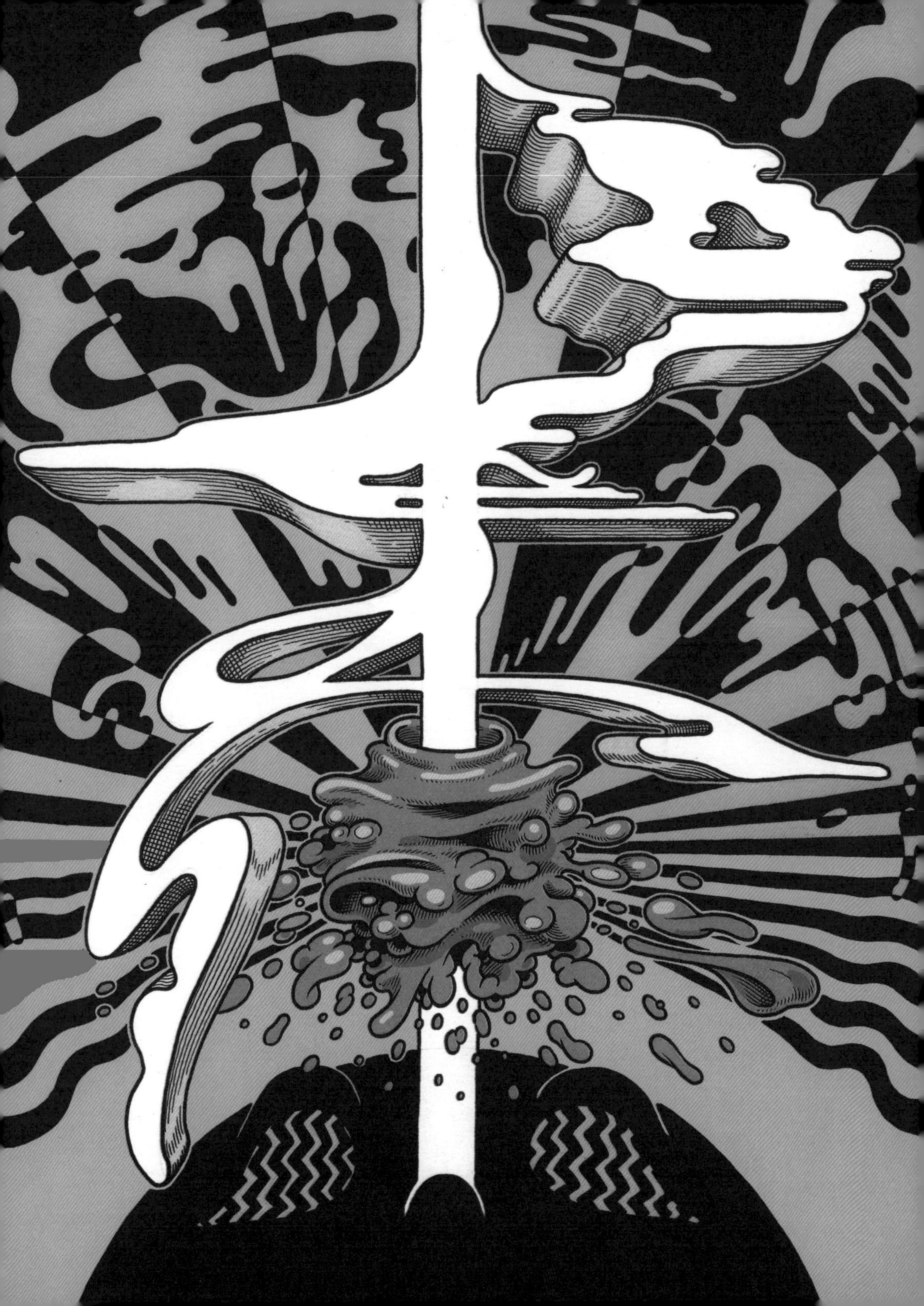

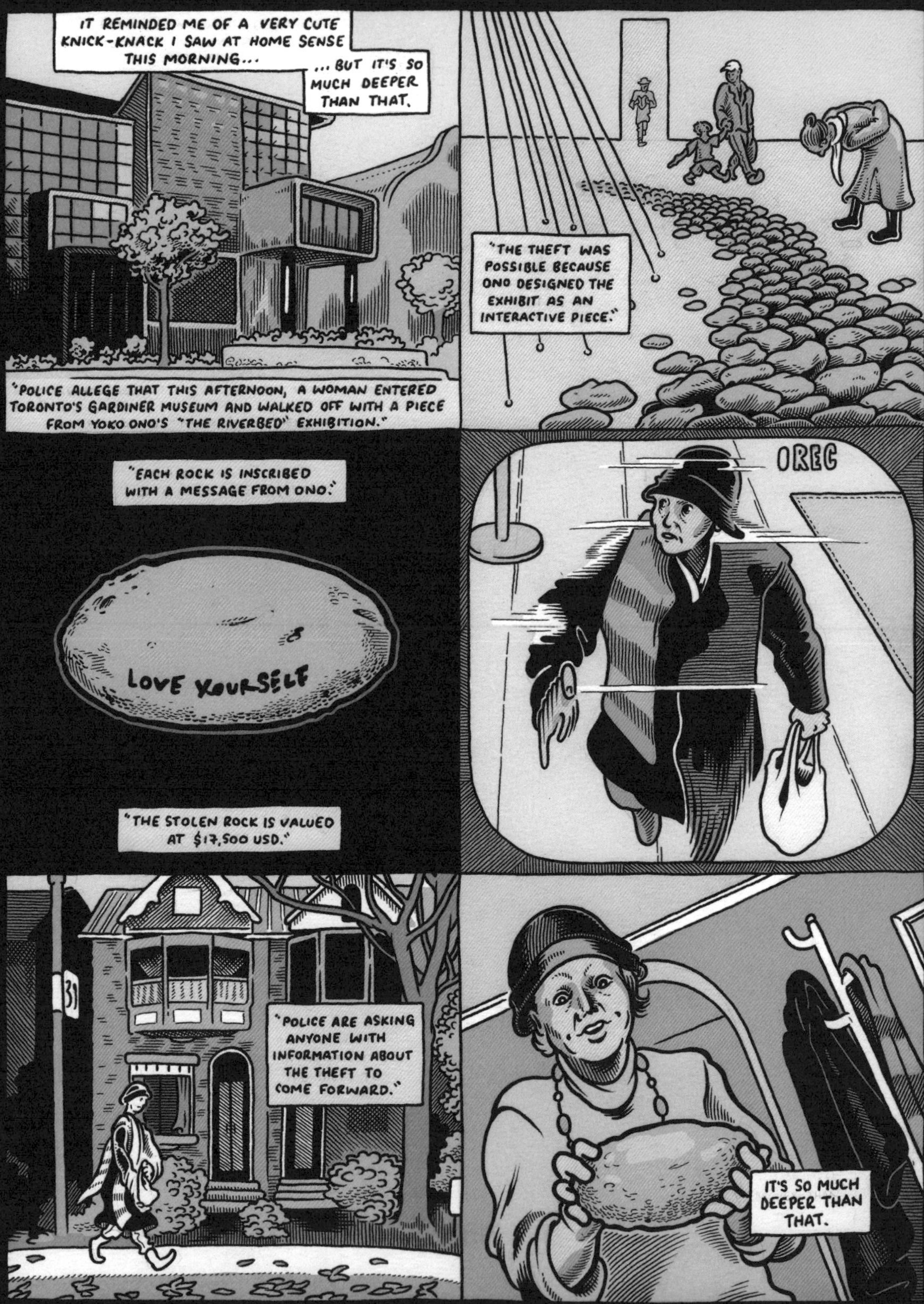
IT REMINDED ME OF A VERY CUTE KNICK-KNACK I SAW AT HOME SENSE THIS MORNING...
... BUT IT'S SO MUCH DEEPER THAN THAT.
"POLICE ALLEGE THAT THIS AFTERNOON, A WOMAN ENTERED TORONTO'S GARDINER MUSEUM AND WALKED OFF WITH A PIECE FROM YOKO ONO'S "THE RIVERBED" EXHIBITION."
"THE THEFT WAS POSSIBLE BECAUSE ONO DESIGNED THE EXHIBIT AS AN INTERACTIVE PIECE."
"EACH ROCK IS INSCRIBED WITH A MESSAGE FROM ONO."
LOVE YOURSELF
"THE STOLEN ROCK IS VALUED AT $17,500 USD."
REC
31
"POLICE ARE ASKING ANYONE WITH INFORMATION ABOUT THE THEFT TO COME FORWARD."
IT'S SO MUCH DEEPER THAN THAT.

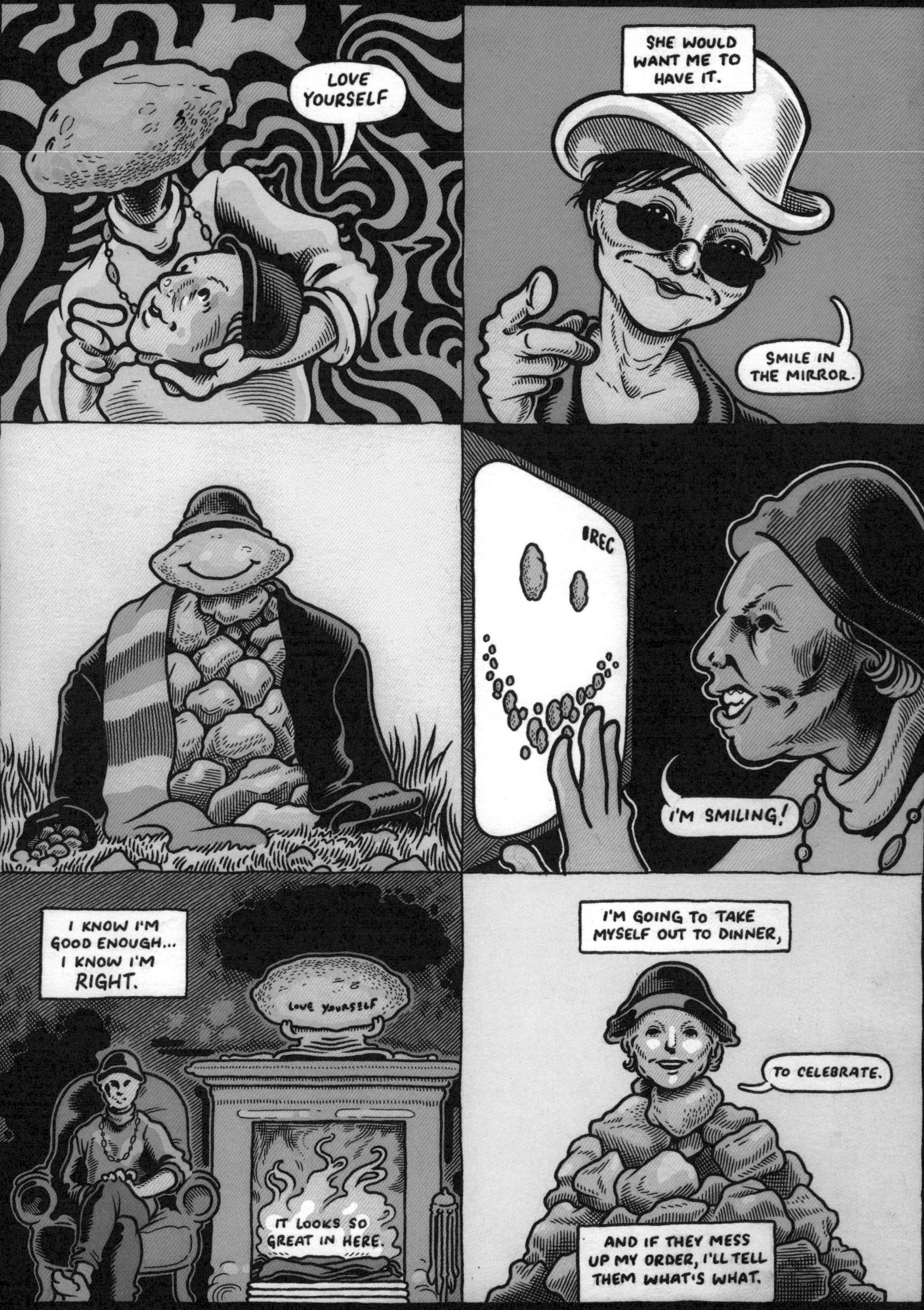
LOVE YOURSELF
SHE WOULD WANT ME TO HAVE IT.
SMILE IN THE MIRROR.
REC
I'M SMILING!
I KNOW I'M GOOD ENOUGH... I KNOW I'M RIGHT.
LOVE YOURSELF
IT LOOKS SO GREAT IN HERE.
I'M GOING TO TAKE MYSELF OUT TO DINNER,
TO CELEBRATE.
AND IF THEY MESS UP MY ORDER, I'LL TELL THEM WHAT'S WHAT.

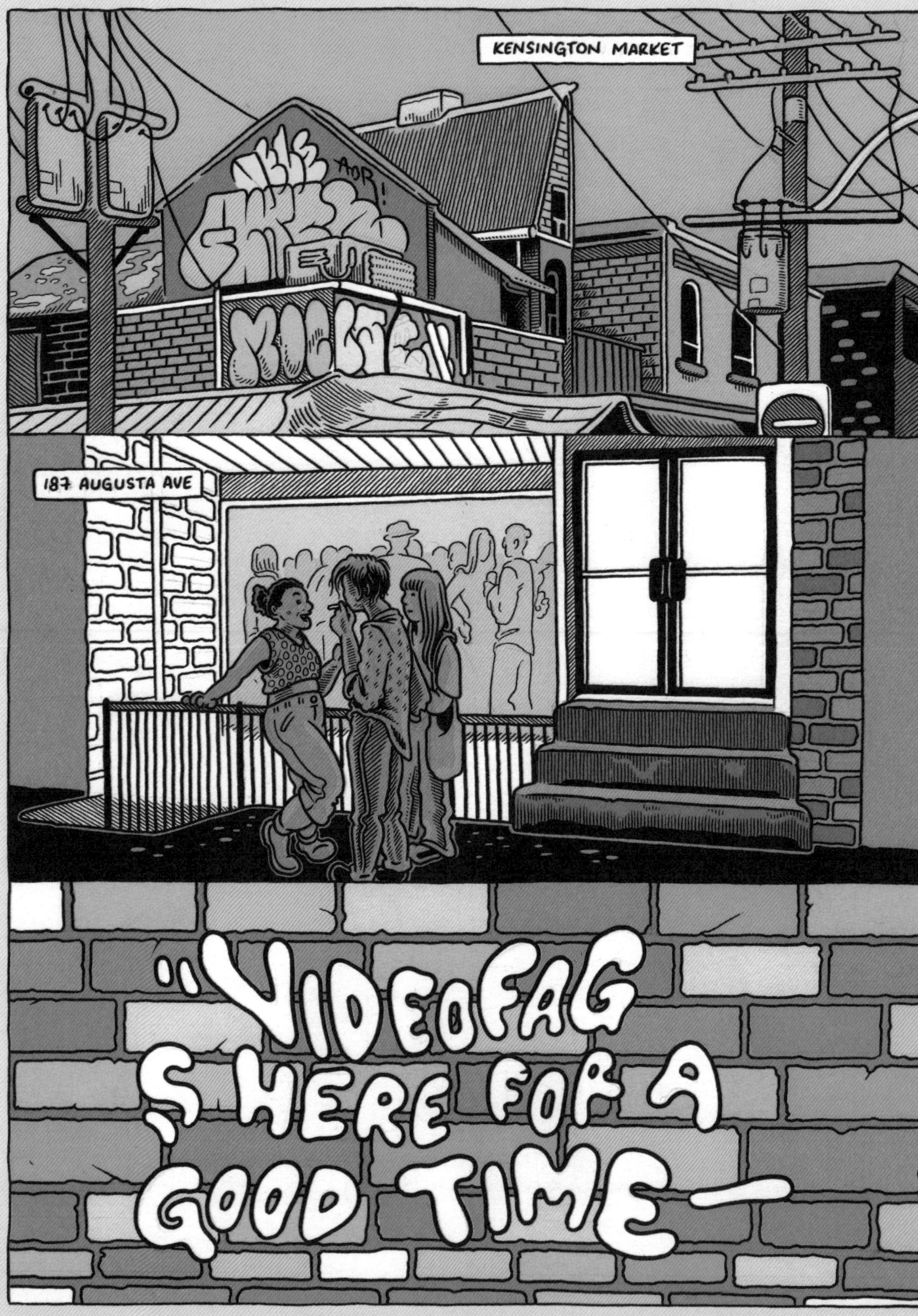
KENSINGTON MARKET
187 AUGUSTA AVE
"VIDEOFAG
S HERE FOR A
GOOD TIME—

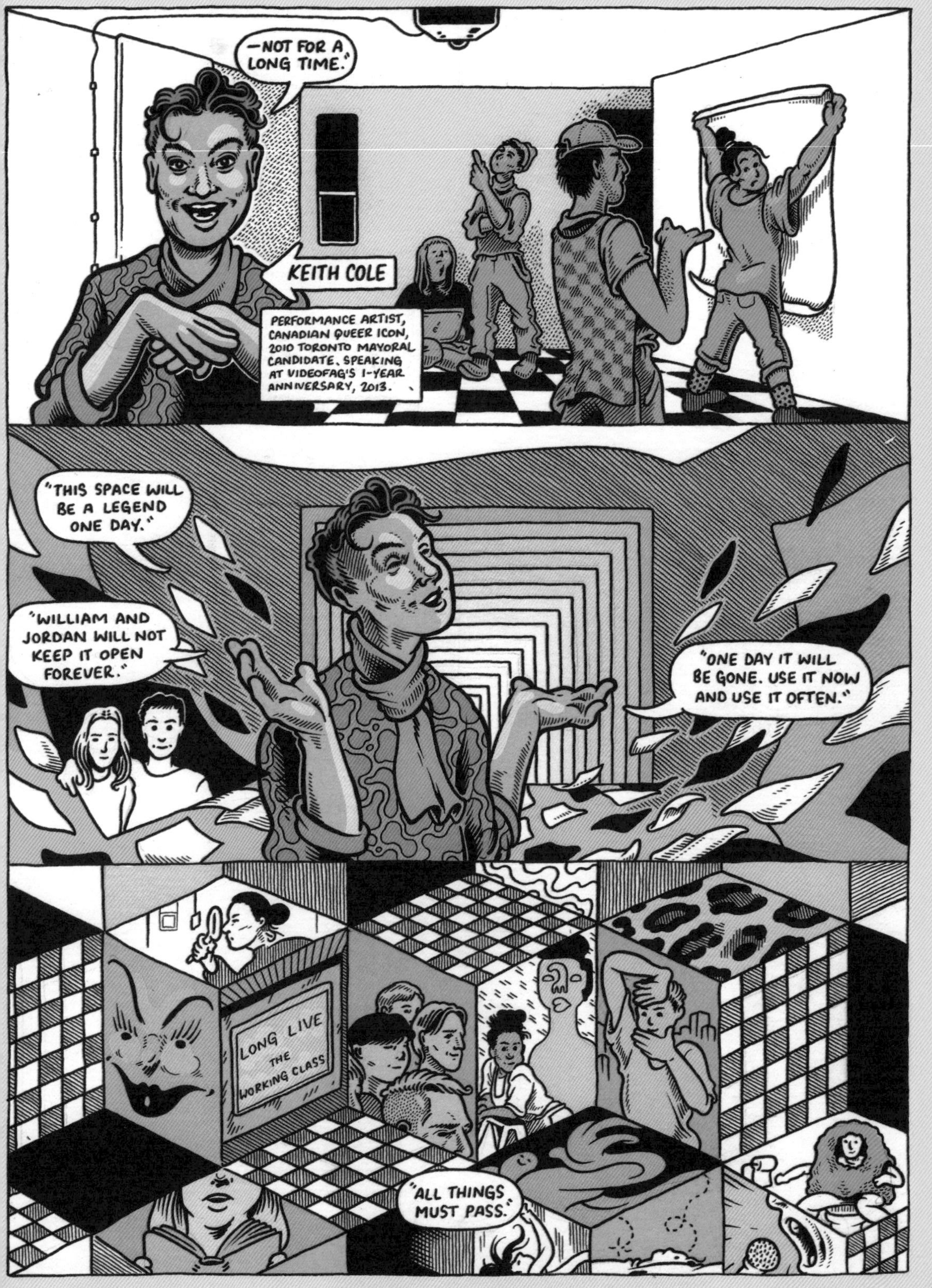
"—NOT FOR A LONG TIME."
KEITH COLE
PERFORMANCE ARTIST, CANADIAN QUEER ICON, 2010 TORONTO MAYORAL CANDIDATE, SPEAKING AT VIDEOFAG'S 1-YEAR ANNIVERSARY, 2013.
"THIS SPACE WILL BE A LEGEND ONE DAY."
"WILLIAM AND JORDAN WILL NOT KEEP IT OPEN FOREVER."
"ONE DAY IT WILL BE GONE. USE IT NOW AND USE IT OFTEN."
LONG LIVE THE WORKING CLASS
"ALL THINGS MUST PASS."

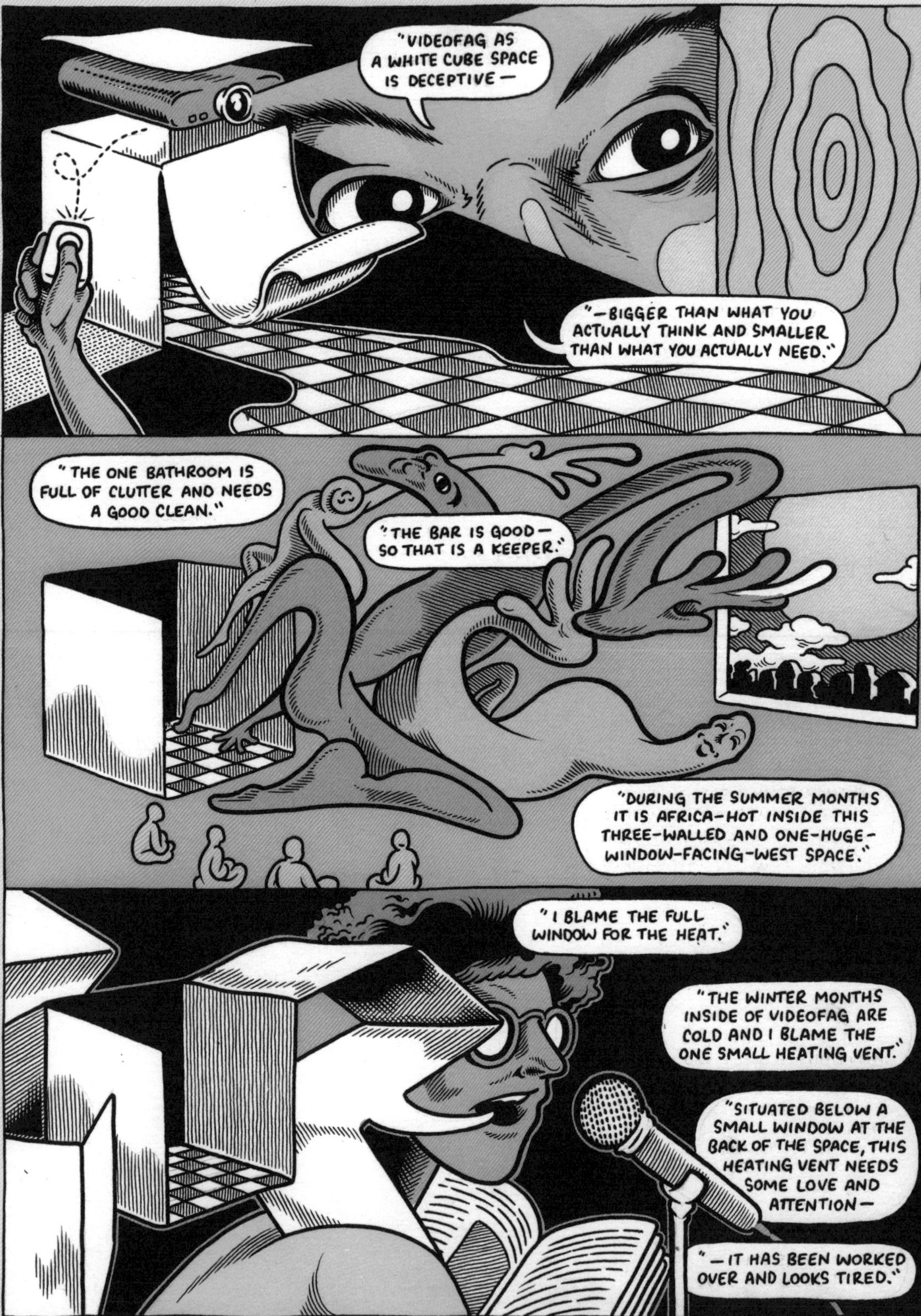
"VIDEOFAG AS A WHITE CUBE SPACE IS DECEPTIVE —
"—BIGGER THAN WHAT YOU ACTUALLY THINK AND SMALLER THAN WHAT YOU ACTUALLY NEED."
"THE ONE BATHROOM IS FULL OF CLUTTER AND NEEDS A GOOD CLEAN."
"THE BAR IS GOOD — SO THAT IS A KEEPER."
"DURING THE SUMMER MONTHS IT IS AFRICA-HOT INSIDE THIS THREE-WALLED AND ONE-HUGE-WINDOW-FACING-WEST SPACE."
"I BLAME THE FULL WINDOW FOR THE HEAT."
"THE WINTER MONTHS INSIDE OF VIDEOFAG ARE COLD AND I BLAME THE ONE SMALL HEATING VENT."
"SITUATED BELOW A SMALL WINDOW AT THE BACK OF THE SPACE, THIS HEATING VENT NEEDS SOME LOVE AND ATTENTION —
"— IT HAS BEEN WORKED OVER AND LOOKS TIRED."

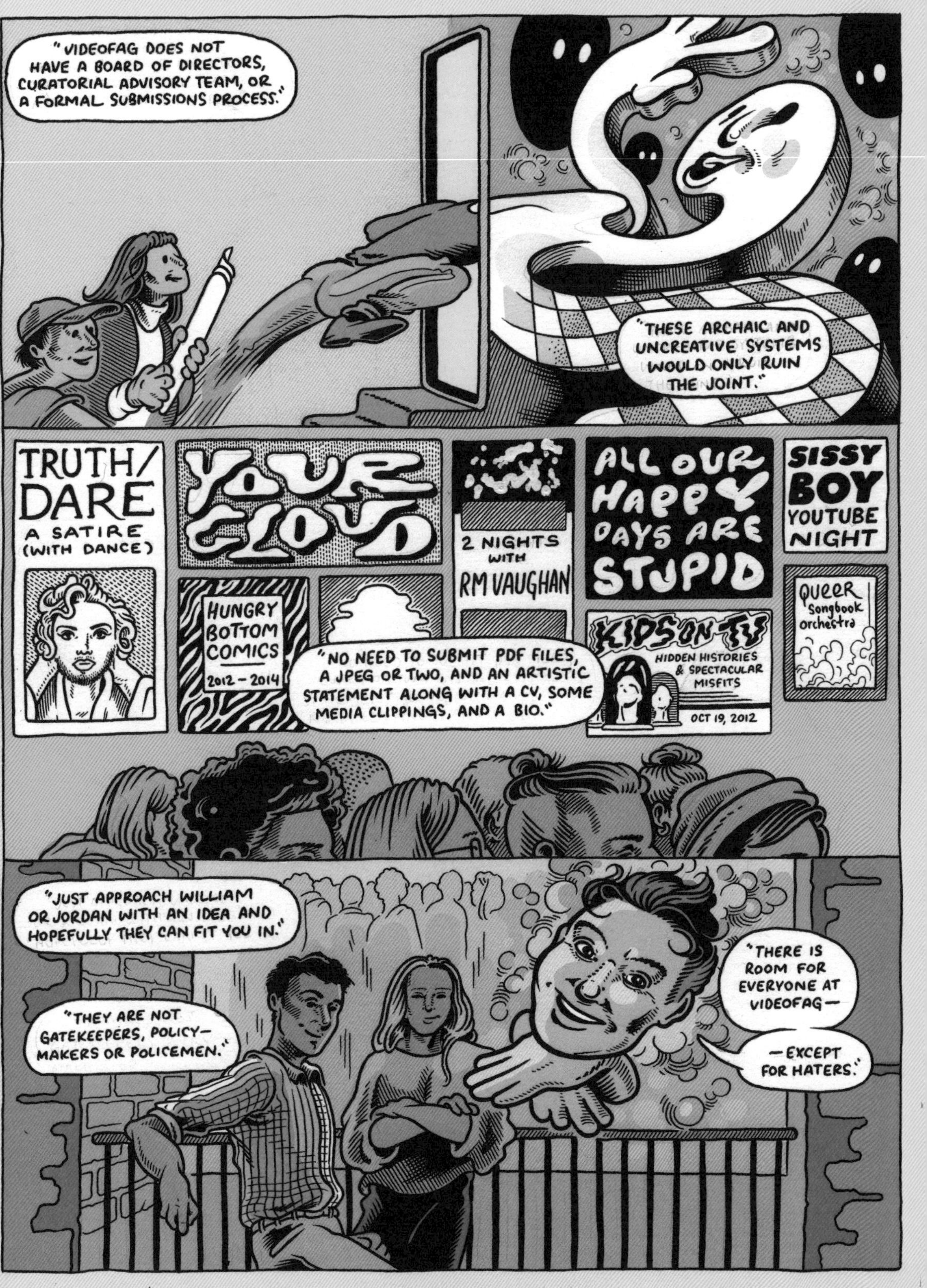
"VIDEOFAG DOES NOT HAVE A BOARD OF DIRECTORS, CURATORIAL ADVISORY TEAM, OR A FORMAL SUBMISSIONS PROCESS."
"THESE ARCHAIC AND UNCREATIVE SYSTEMS WOULD ONLY RUIN THE JOINT."
TRUTH/ DARE A SATIRE (WITH DANCE)
YOUR CLOUD
2 NIGHTS WITH RM VAUGHAN
ALL OUR HAPPY DAYS ARE STUPID
SISSY BOY YOUTUBE NIGHT
HUNGRY BOTTOM COMICS 2012 – 2014
"NO NEED TO SUBMIT PDF FILES, A JPEG OR TWO, AND AN ARTISTIC STATEMENT ALONG WITH A CV, SOME MEDIA CLIPPINGS, AND A BIO."
KIDS ON TV HIDDEN HISTORIES & SPECTACULAR MISFITS OCT 19, 2012
Queer Songbook orchestra
"JUST APPROACH WILLIAM OR JORDAN WITH AN IDEA AND HOPEFULLY THEY CAN FIT YOU IN."
"THEY ARE NOT GATEKEEPERS, POLICY-MAKERS OR POLICEMEN."
"THERE IS ROOM FOR EVERYONE AT VIDEOFAG—
—EXCEPT FOR HATERS."

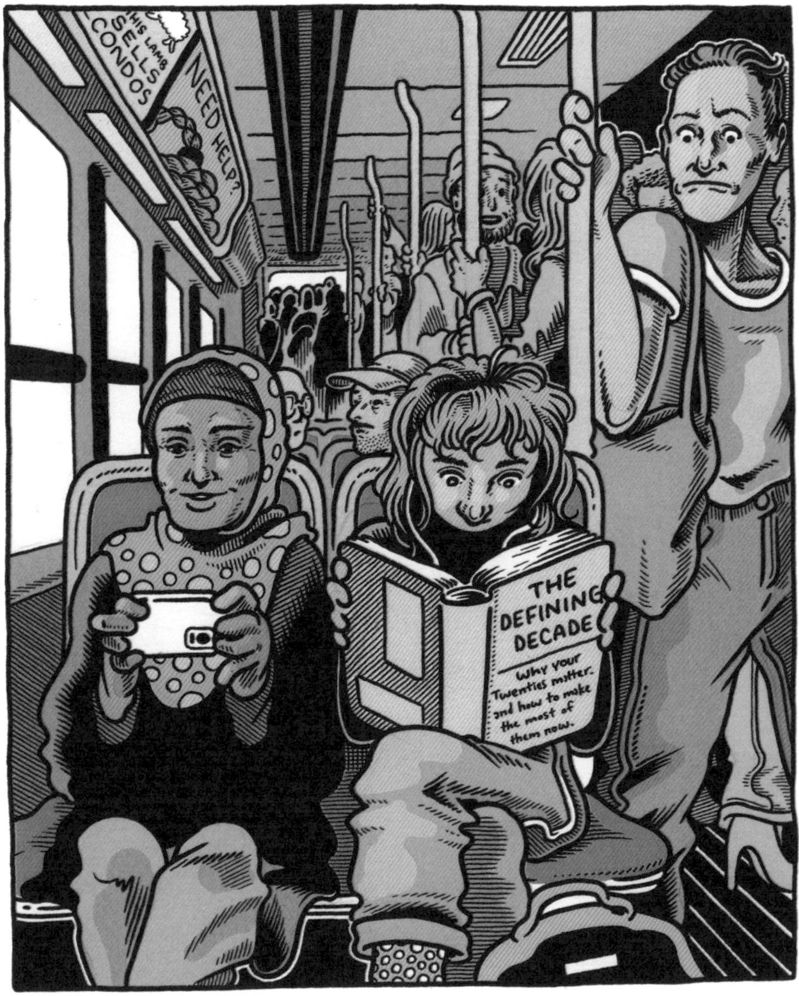
HIS LAMB SELLS CONDOS
NEED HELP?
THE DEFINING DECADE
Why your Twenties matter. and how to make the most of them now.

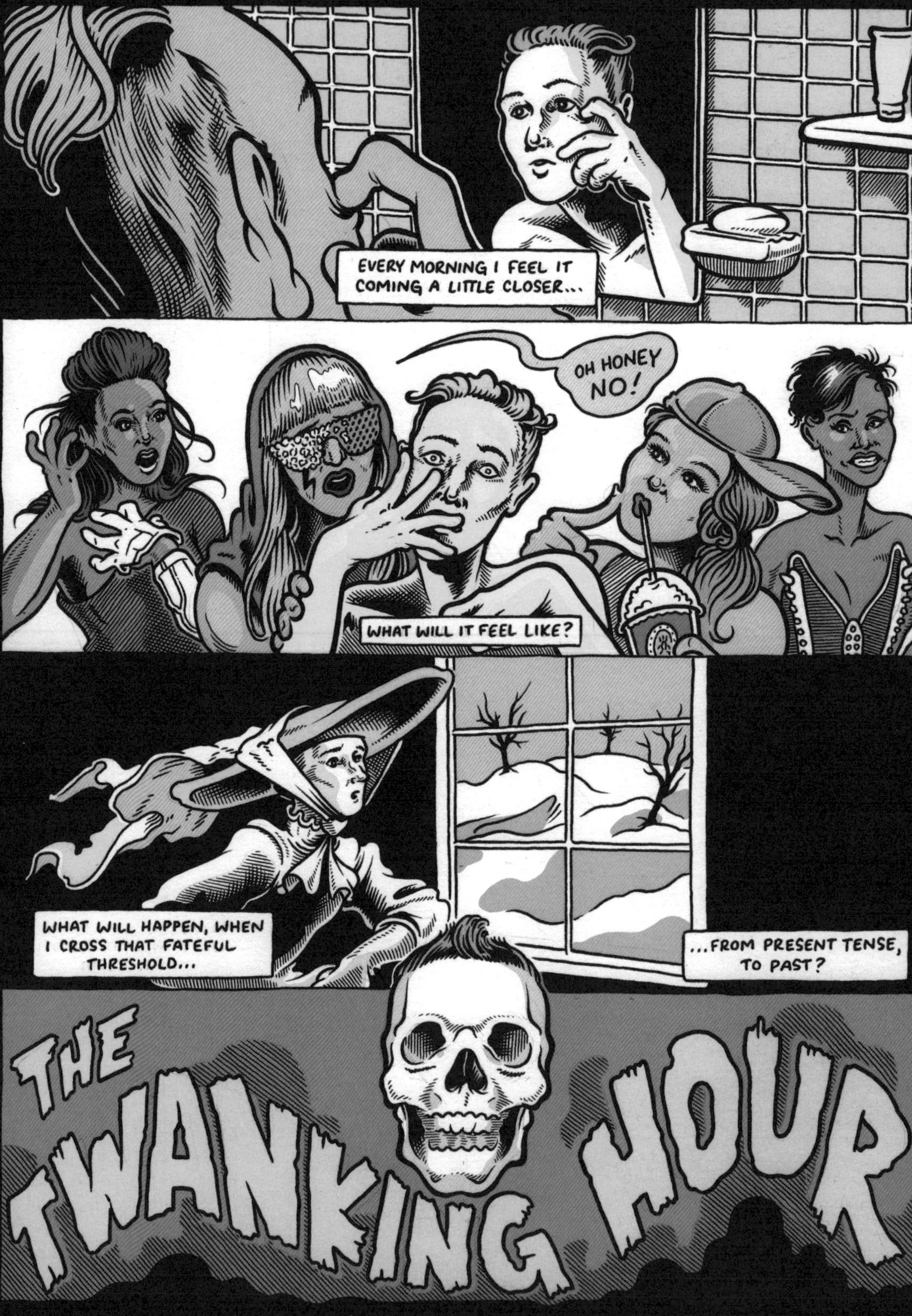
EVERY MORNING I FEEL IT COMING A LITTLE CLOSER...
OH HONEY NO!
WHAT WILL IT FEEL LIKE?
WHAT WILL HAPPEN, WHEN I CROSS THAT FATEFUL THRESHOLD...
...FROM PRESENT TENSE, TO PAST?
THE TWANKING HOUR

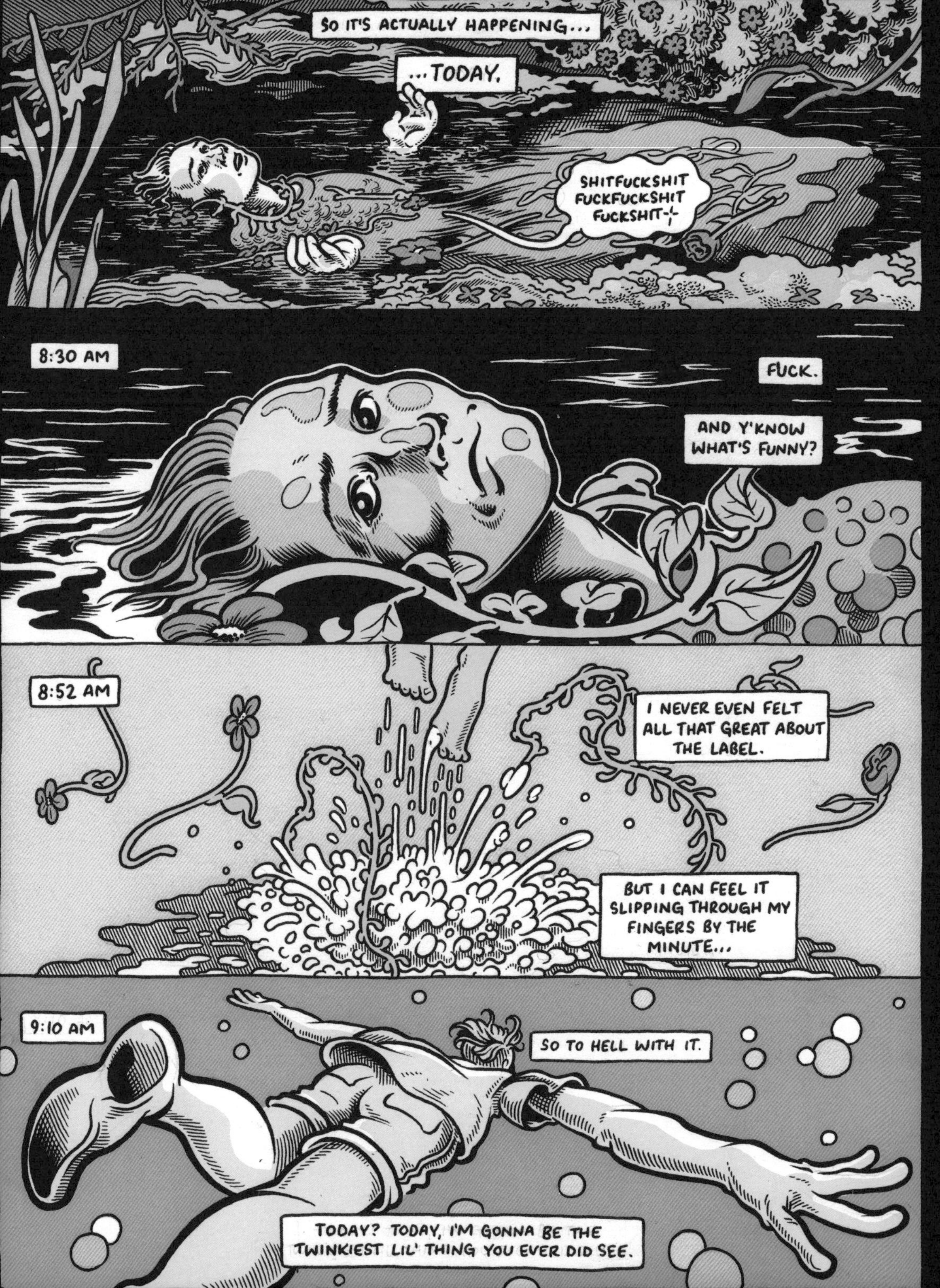
SO IT'S ACTUALLY HAPPENING...
...TODAY.
SHITFUCKSHIT FUCKFUCKSHIT FUCKSHIT-
8:30 AM
FUCK.
AND Y'KNOW WHAT'S FUNNY?
8:52 AM
I NEVER EVEN FELT ALL THAT GREAT ABOUT THE LABEL.
BUT I CAN FEEL IT SLIPPING THROUGH MY FINGERS BY THE MINUTE...
9:10 AM
SO TO HELL WITH IT.
TODAY? TODAY, I'M GONNA BE THE TWINKIEST LIL' THING YOU EVER DID SEE.

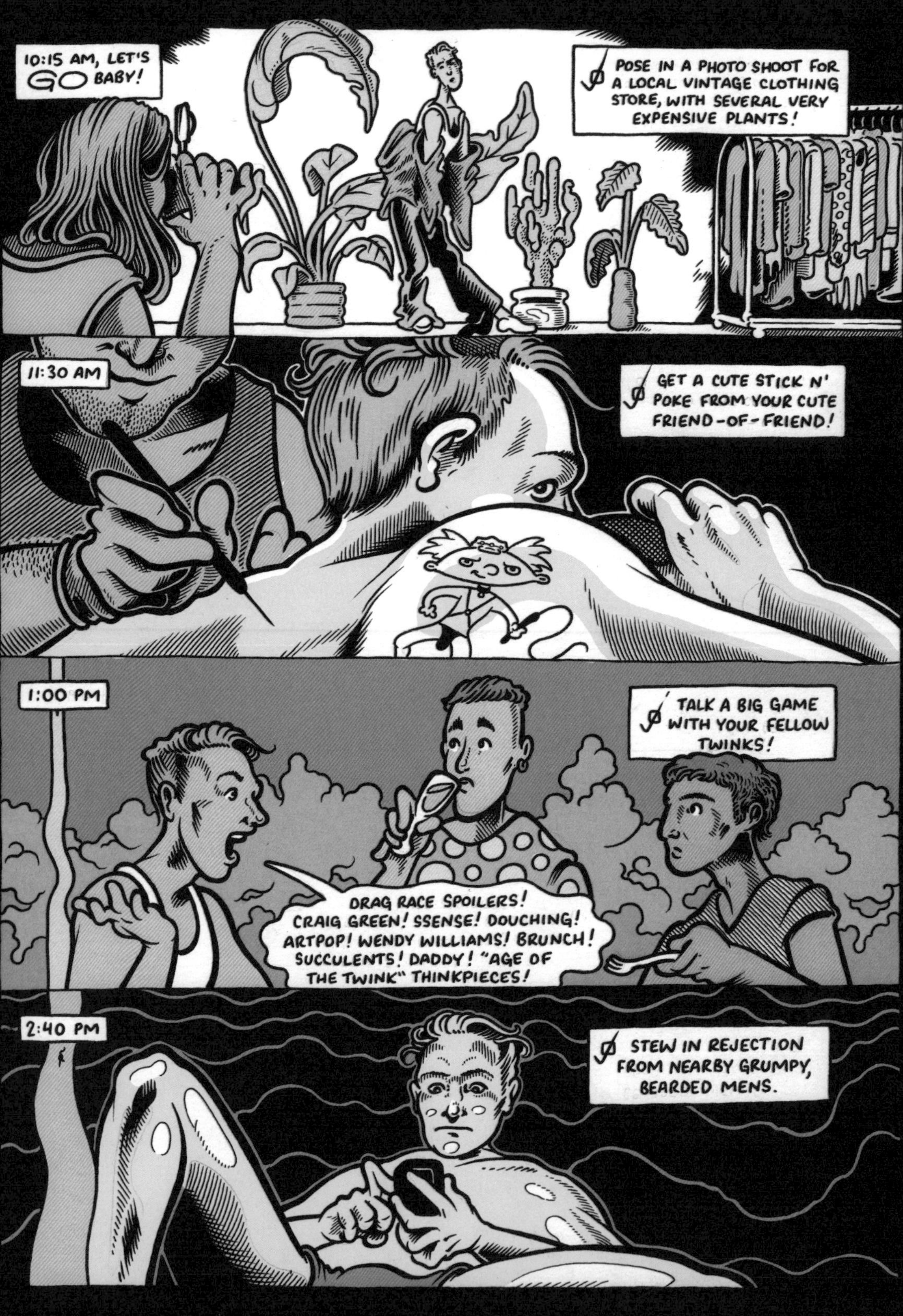
10:15 AM, LET'S GO BABY!
POSE IN A PHOTO SHOOT FOR A LOCAL VINTAGE CLOTHING STORE, WITH SEVERAL VERY EXPENSIVE PLANTS!
11:30 AM
GET A CUTE STICK N' POKE FROM YOUR CUTE FRIEND-OF-FRIEND!
1:00 PM
TALK A BIG GAME WITH YOUR FELLOW TWINKS!
DRAG RACE SPOILERS! CRAIG GREEN! SSENSE! DOUCHING! ARTPOP! WENDY WILLIAMS! BRUNCH! SUCCULENTS! DADDY! "AGE OF THE TWINK" THINKPIECES!
2:40 PM
STEW IN REJECTION FROM NEARBY GRUMPY, BEARDED MENS.

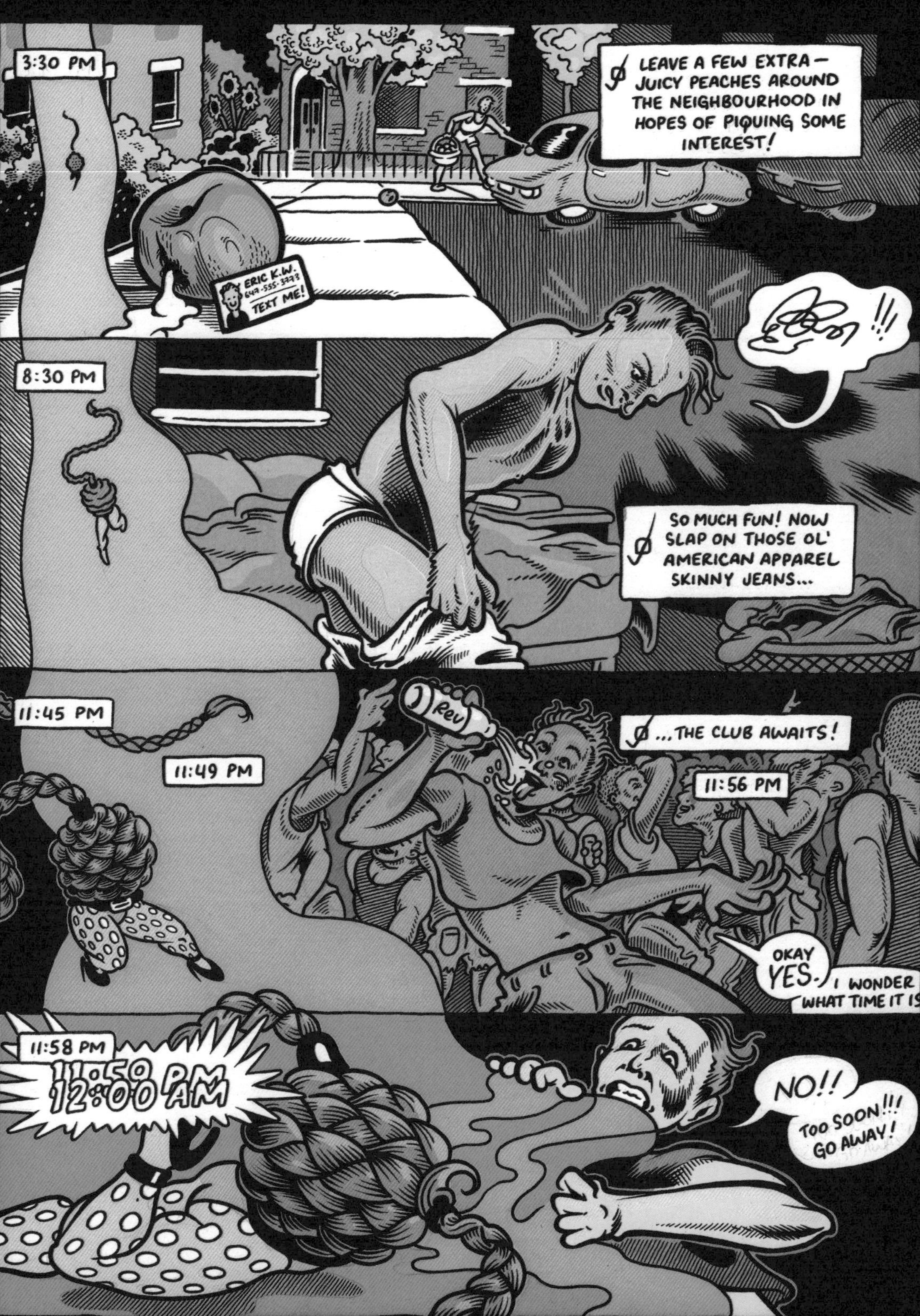
3:30 PM
LEAVE A FEW EXTRA-JUICY PEACHES AROUND THE NEIGHBOURHOOD IN HOPES OF PIQUING SOME INTEREST!
ERIC K.W.
647-555-3773
TEXT ME!
!!!
8:30 PM
SO MUCH FUN! NOW SLAP ON THOSE OL' AMERICAN APPAREL SKINNY JEANS...
11:45 PM
Rev
...THE CLUB AWAITS!
11:49 PM
11:56 PM
OKAY YES.
I WONDER WHAT TIME IT IS
11:58 PM
11:59 PM
12:00 AM
NO!!
TOO SOON!!! GO AWAY!

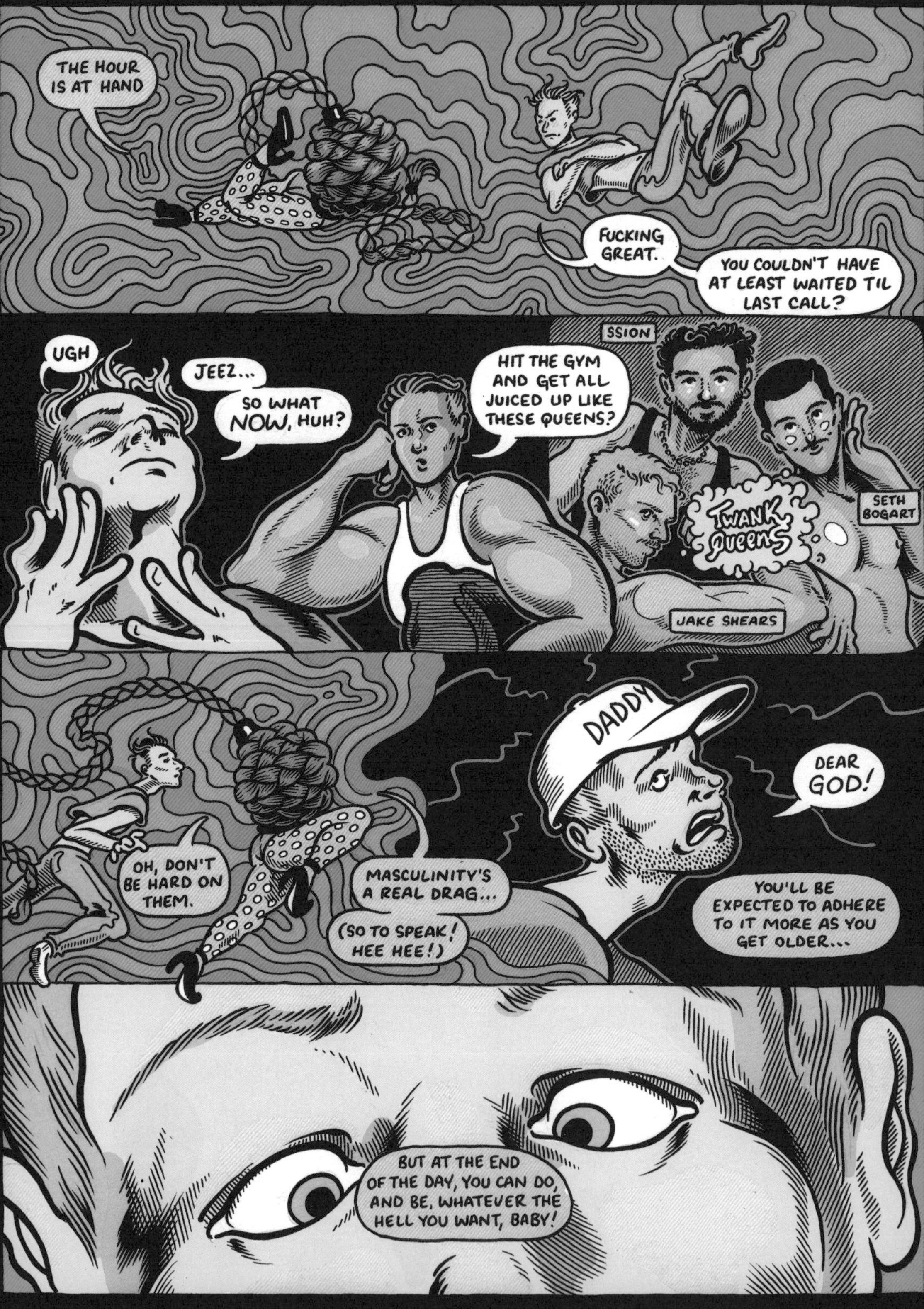

THE HOUR IS AT HAND
FUCKING GREAT.
YOU COULDN'T HAVE AT LEAST WAITED TIL LAST CALL?
UGH
JEEZ...
SO WHAT NOW, HUH?
HIT THE GYM AND GET ALL JUICED UP LIKE THESE QUEENS?
SSION
SETH BOGART
TWANK QUEENS
JAKE SHEARS
DADDY
DEAR GOD!
OH, DON'T BE HARD ON THEM.
MASCULINITY'S A REAL DRAG...
(SO TO SPEAK! HEE HEE!)
YOU'LL BE EXPECTED TO ADHERE TO IT MORE AS YOU GET OLDER...
BUT AT THE END OF THE DAY, YOU CAN DO, AND BE, WHATEVER THE HELL YOU WANT, BABY!

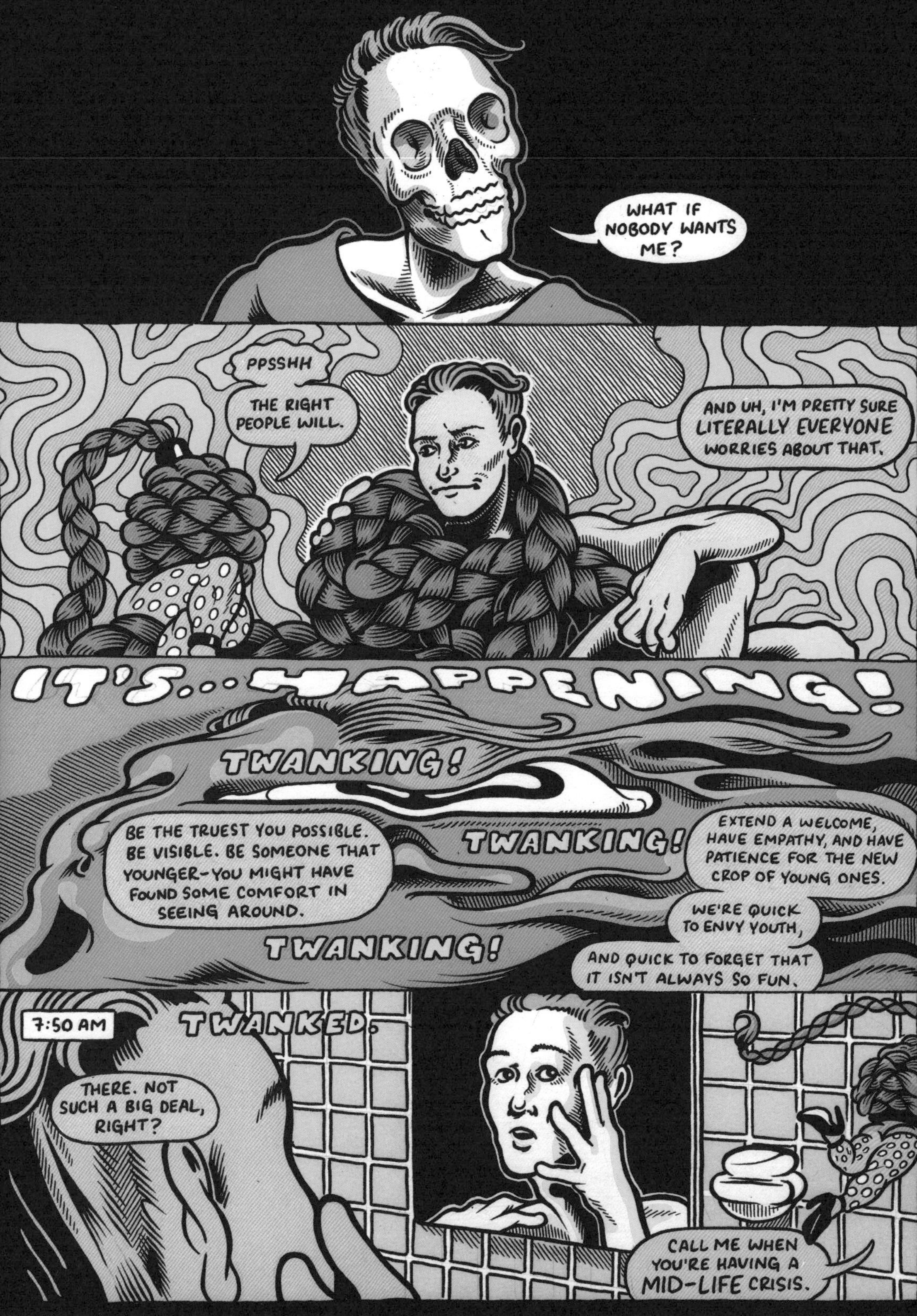
WHAT IF NOBODY WANTS ME?
PPSSHH
THE RIGHT PEOPLE WILL.
AND UH, I'M PRETTY SURE LITERALLY EVERYONE WORRIES ABOUT THAT.
IT'S...HAPPENING!
TWANKING!
BE THE TRUEST YOU POSSIBLE. BE VISIBLE. BE SOMEONE THAT YOUNGER-YOU MIGHT HAVE FOUND SOME COMFORT IN SEEING AROUND.
TWANKING!
EXTEND A WELCOME, HAVE EMPATHY, AND HAVE PATIENCE FOR THE NEW CROP OF YOUNG ONES.
WE'RE QUICK TO ENVY YOUTH,
TWANKING!
AND QUICK TO FORGET THAT IT ISN'T ALWAYS SO FUN.
7:50 AM
TWANKED.
THERE. NOT SUCH A BIG DEAL, RIGHT?
CALL ME WHEN YOU'RE HAVING A MID-LIFE CRISIS.

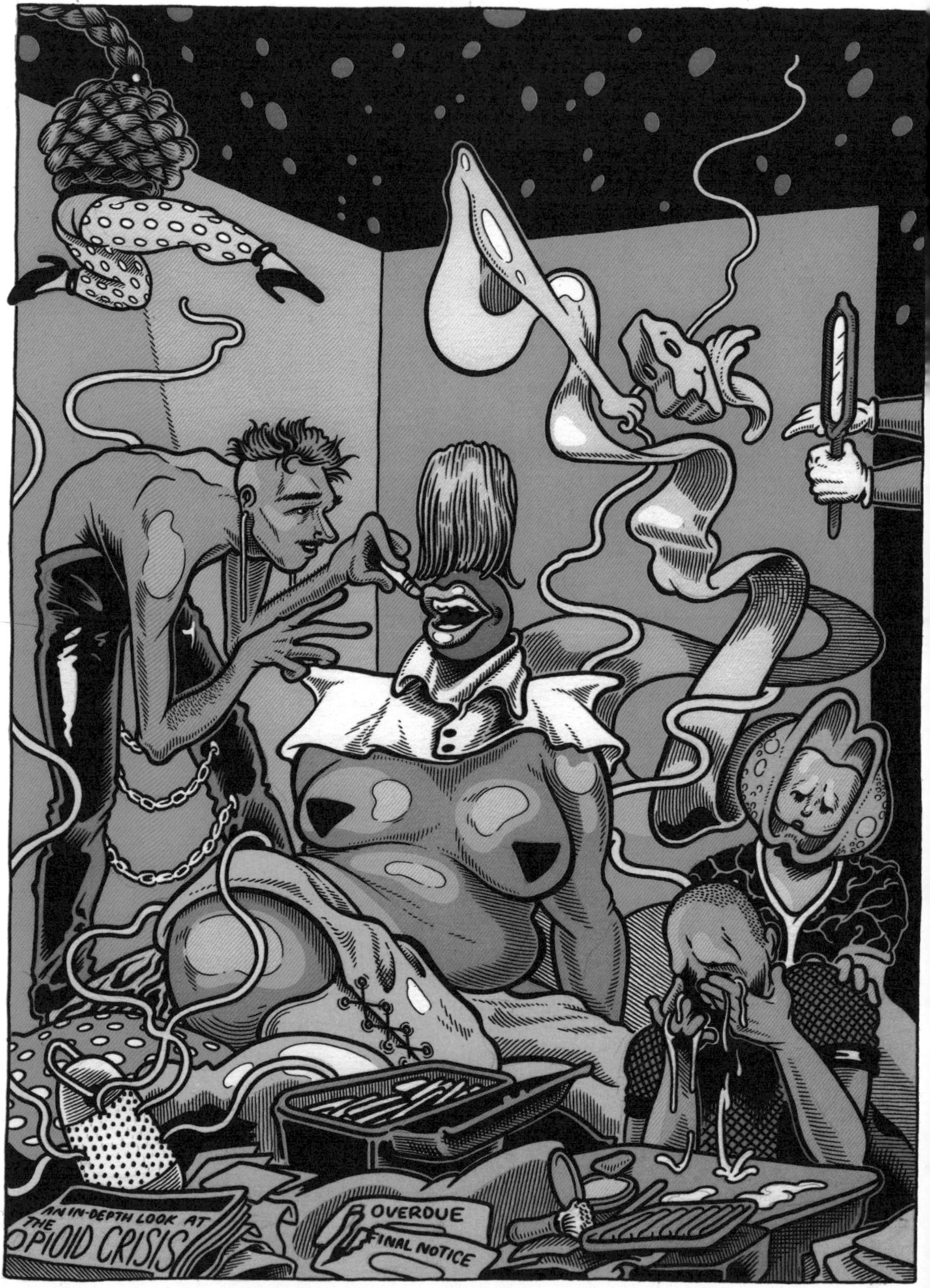
AN IN-DEPTH LOOK AT THE OPIOID CRISIS
OVERDUE
FINAL NOTICE

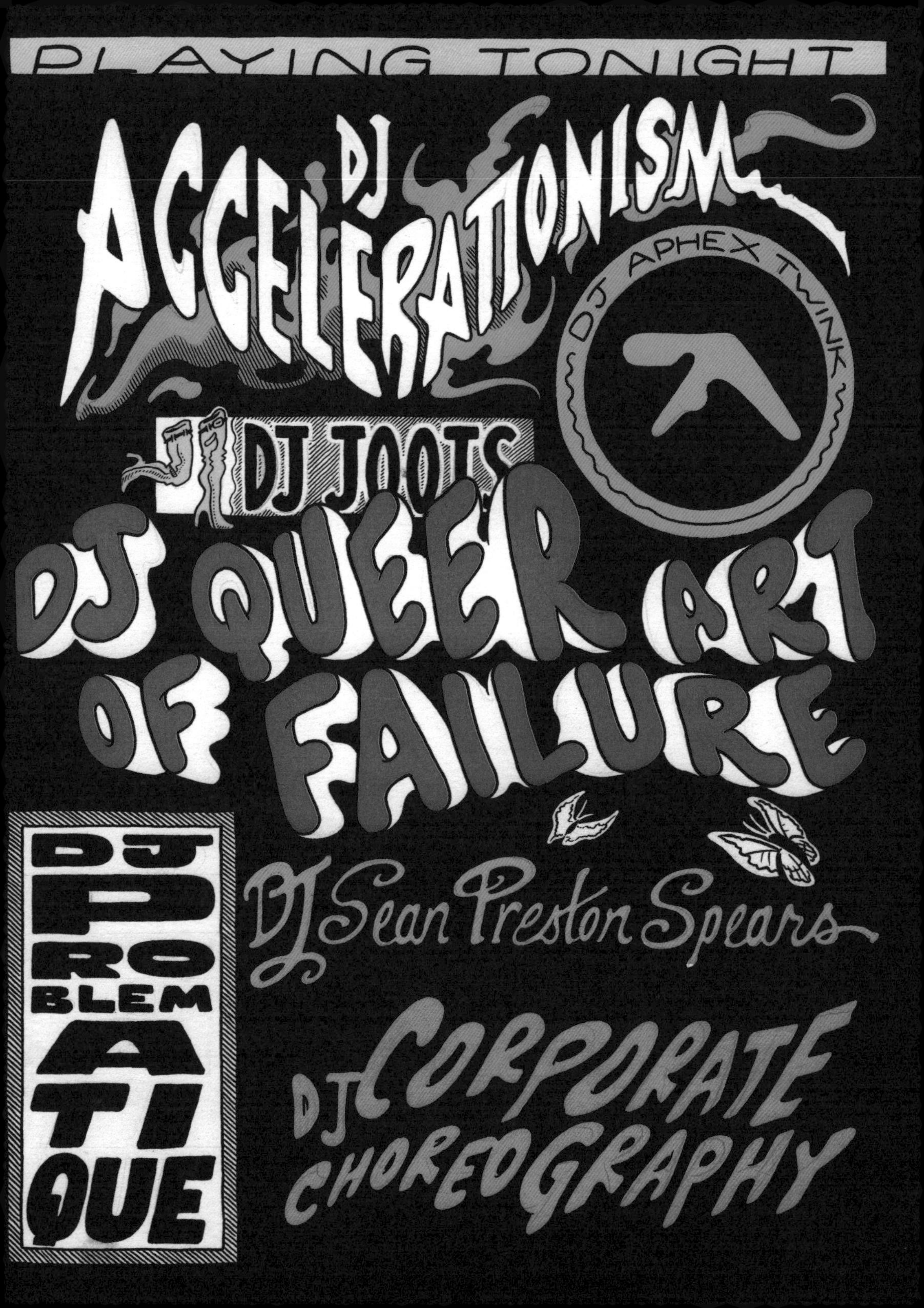
PLAYING TONIGHT
DJ ACCELERATIONISM
DJ APHEX TWINK
DJ JOOTS
DJ QUEER ART OF FAILURE
DJ Sean Preston Spears
DJ PRO BLEM ATI QUE
DJ CORPORATE CHOREOGRAPHY

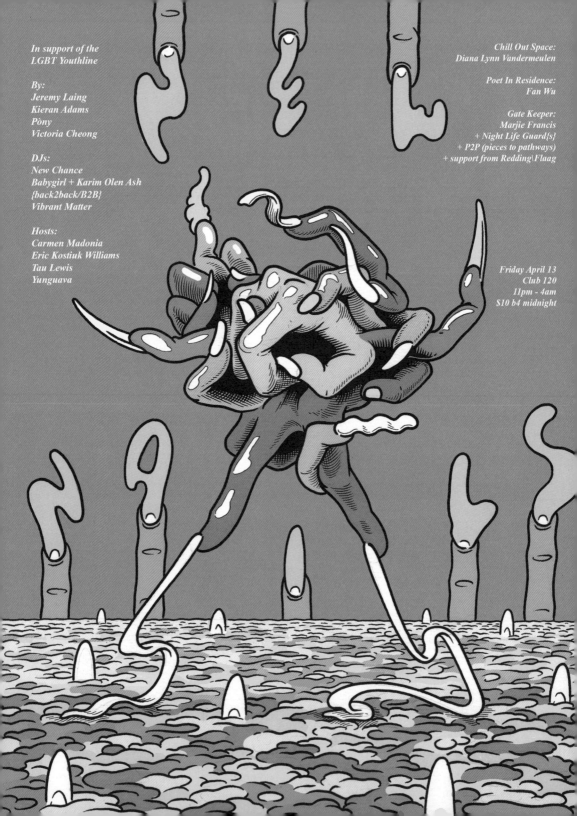

*In support of the
LGBT Youthline*

*By:
Jeremy Laing
Kieran Adams
Pòny
Victoria Cheong*

*DJs:
New Chance
Babygirl + Karim Olen Ash
{back2back/B2B}
Vibrant Matter*

*Hosts:
Carmen Madonia
Eric Kostiuk Williams
Tau Lewis
Yunguava*

*Chill Out Space:
Diana Lynn Vandermeulen*

*Poet In Residence:
Fan Wu*

*Gate Keeper:
Marjie Francis
+ Night Life Guard{s}
+ P2P (pieces to pathways)
+ support from Redding\Flaag*

*Friday April 13
Club 120
11pm - 4am
$10 b4 midnight*

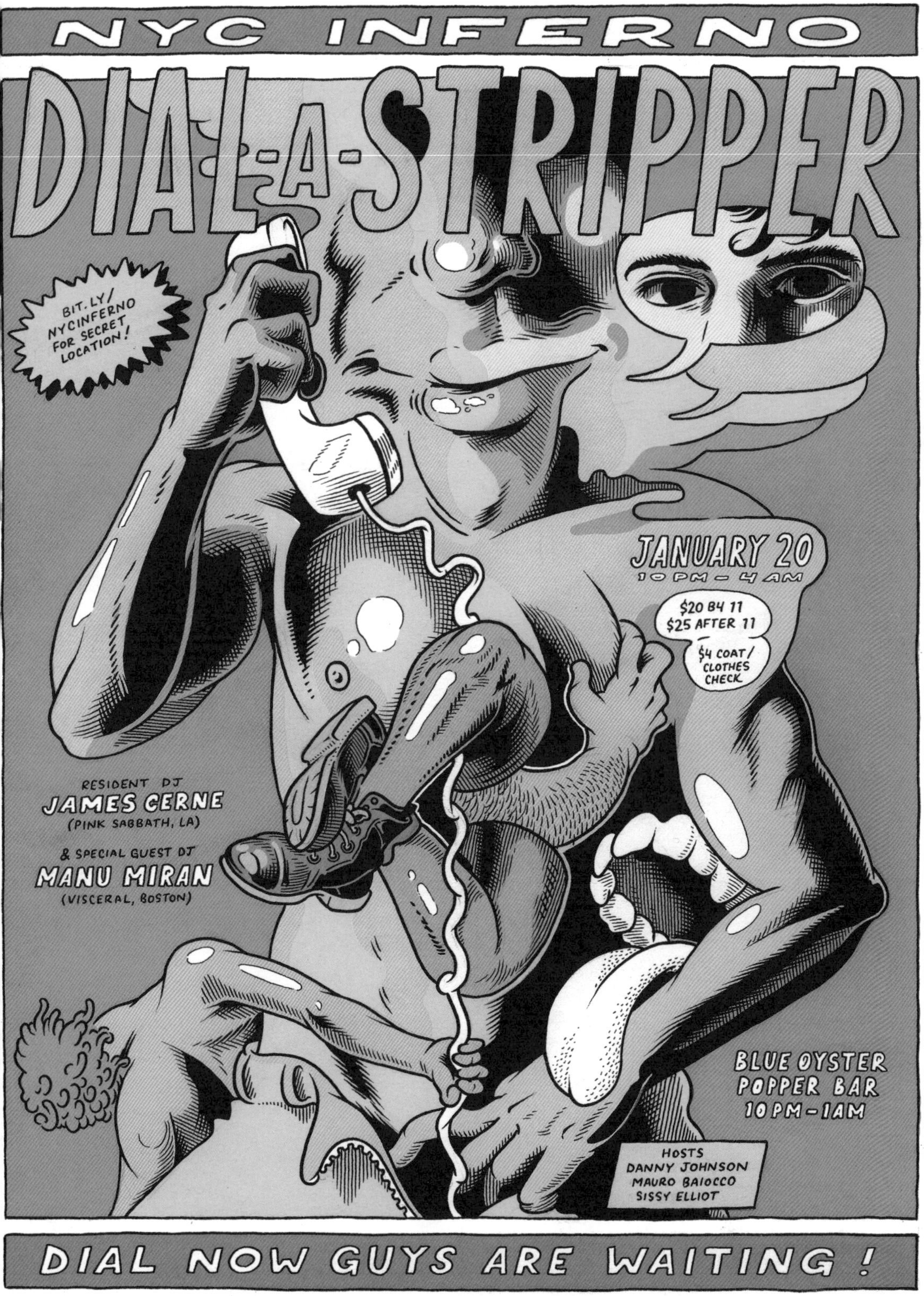
NYC INFERNO
DIAL-A-STRIPPER
BIT.LY/ NYCINFERNO FOR SECRET LOCATION!
JANUARY 20
10PM – 4AM
$20 B4 11
$25 AFTER 11
$4 COAT/ CLOTHES CHECK
RESIDENT DJ
JAMES CERNE
(PINK SABBATH, LA)
& SPECIAL GUEST DJ
MANU MIRAN
(VISCERAL, BOSTON)
BLUE OYSTER POPPER BAR 10PM–1AM
HOSTS
DANNY JOHNSON
MAURO BAIOCCO
SISSY ELLIOT
DIAL NOW GUYS ARE WAITING!

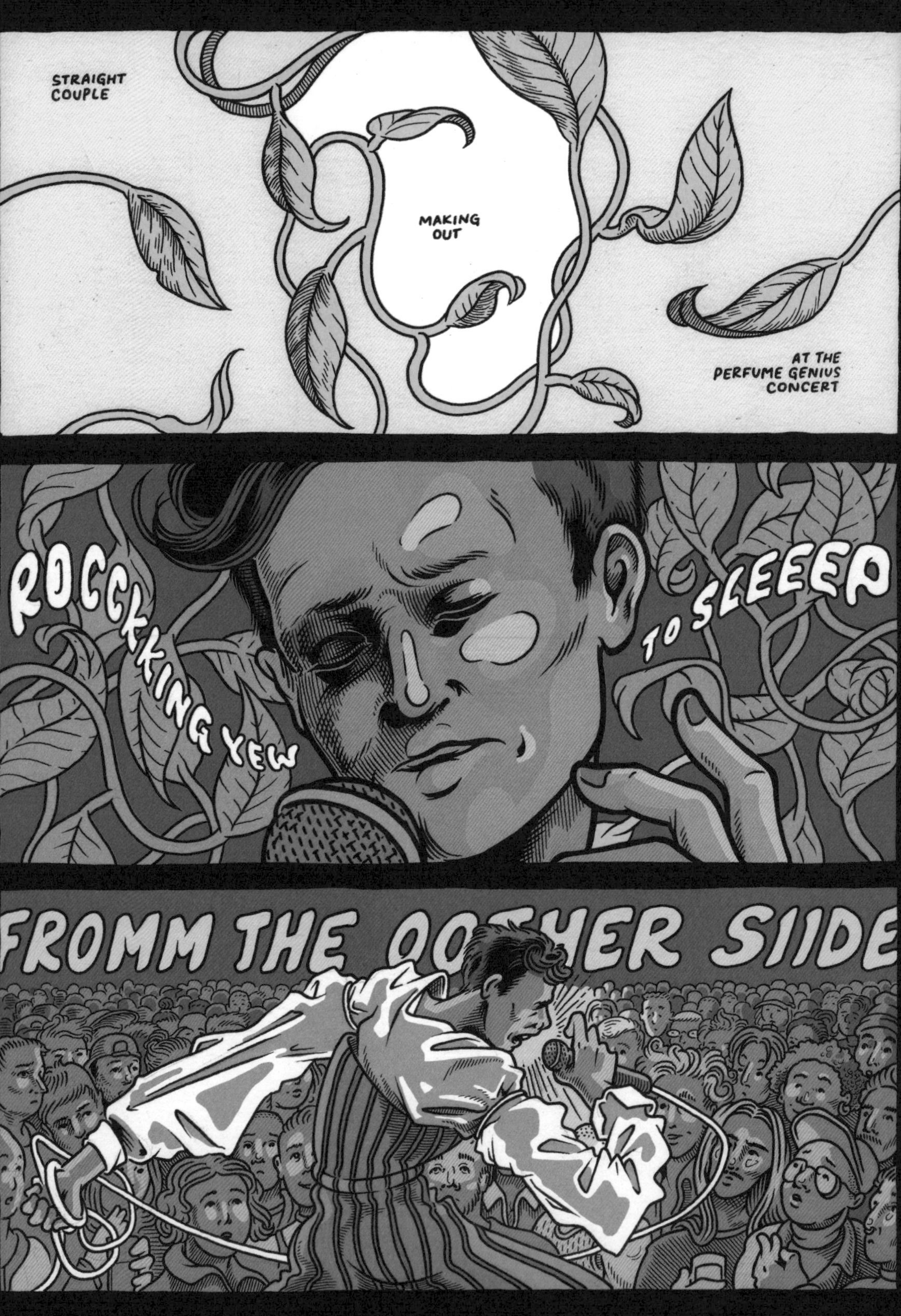
STRAIGHT COUPLE
MAKING OUT
AT THE PERFUME GENIUS CONCERT
ROCCKKING YEW
TO SLEEEP
FROMM THE OOTHER SIIDE

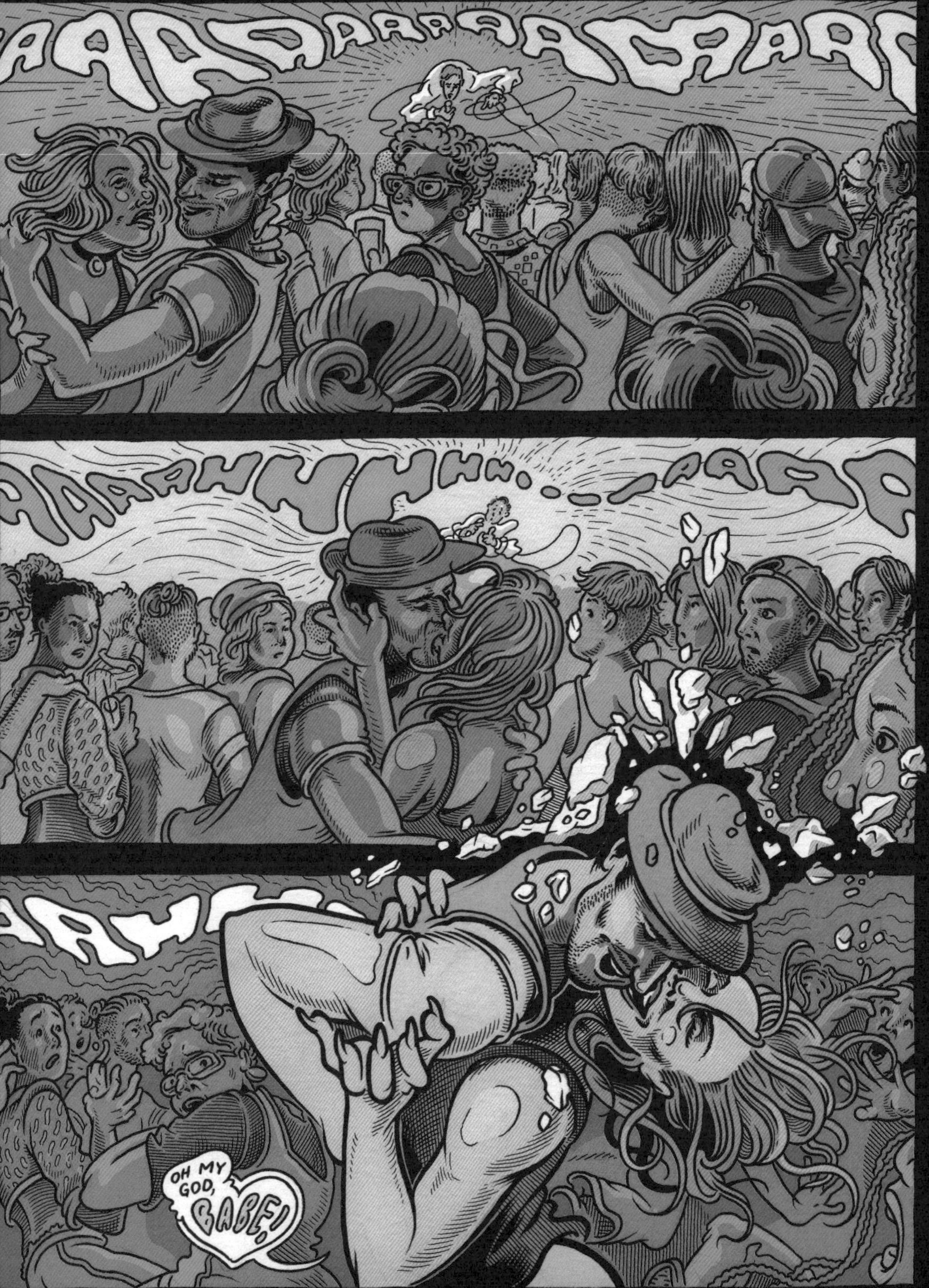
OH MY GOD, BABE!

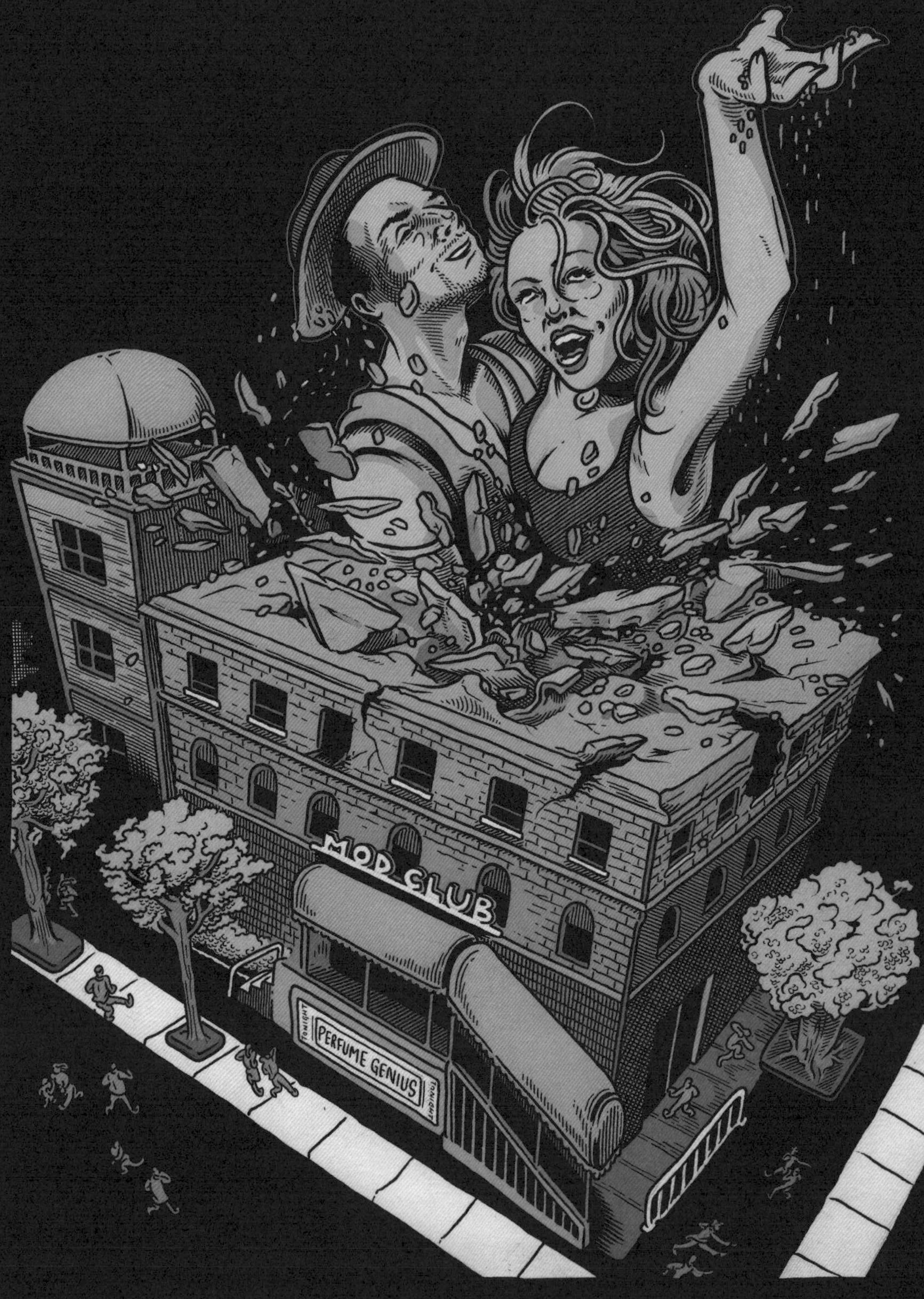

MOD CLUB
TONIGHT
PERFUME GENIUS
TONIGHT

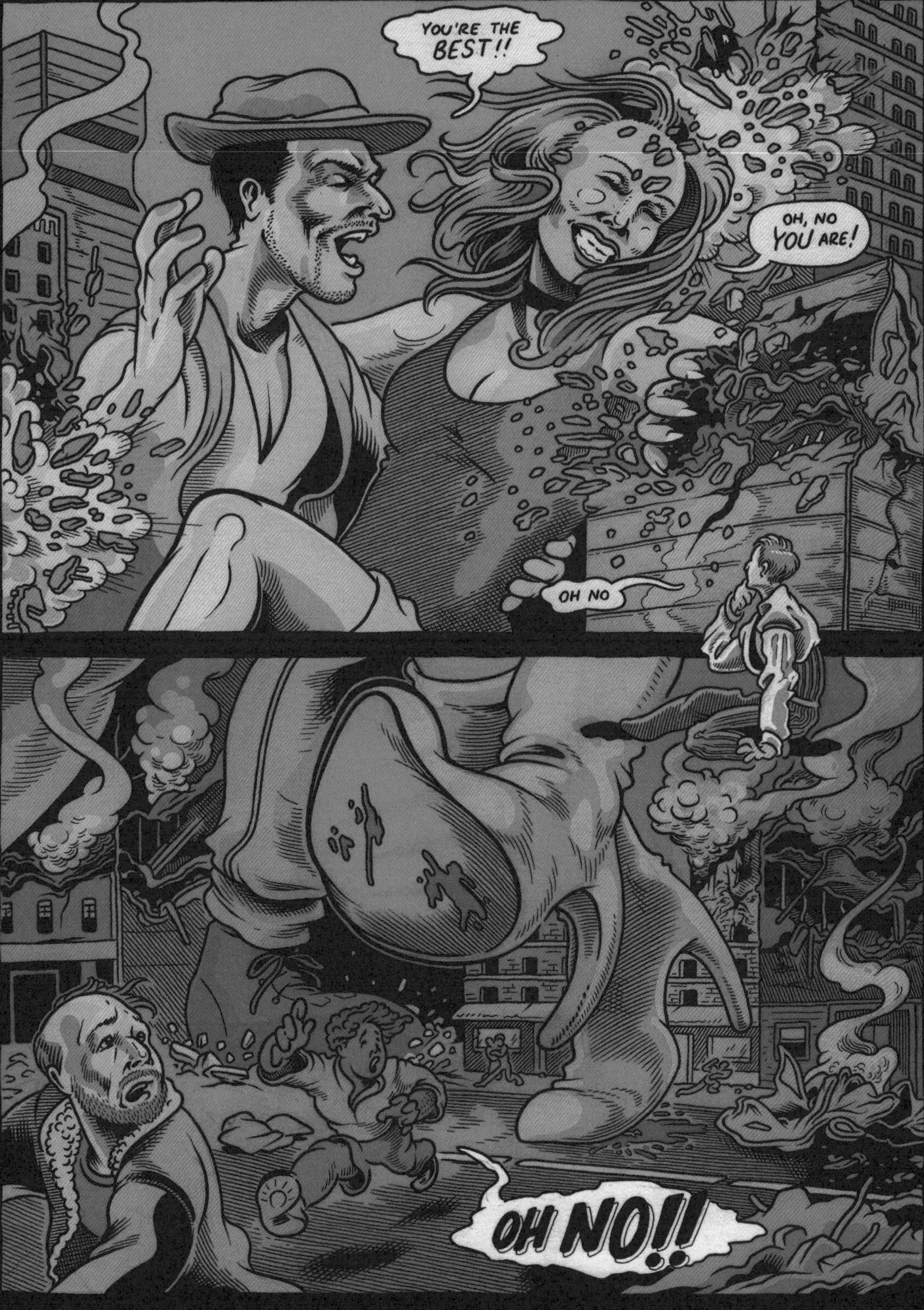
YOU'RE THE BEST!!
OH, NO YOU ARE!
OH NO
OH NO!!

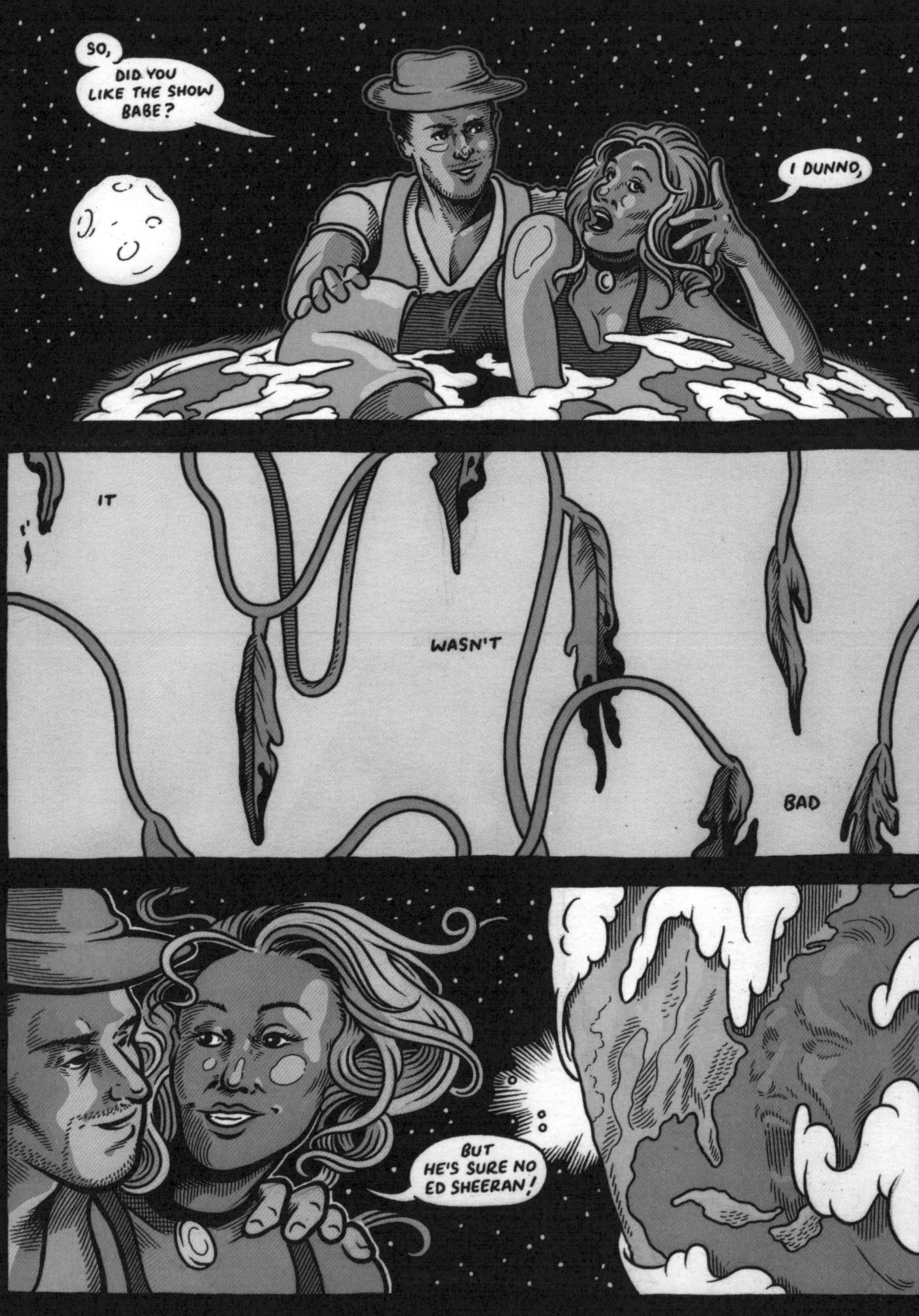
SO,
DID YOU LIKE THE SHOW BABE?
I DUNNO,
IT
WASN'T
BAD
BUT HE'S SURE NO ED SHEERAN!

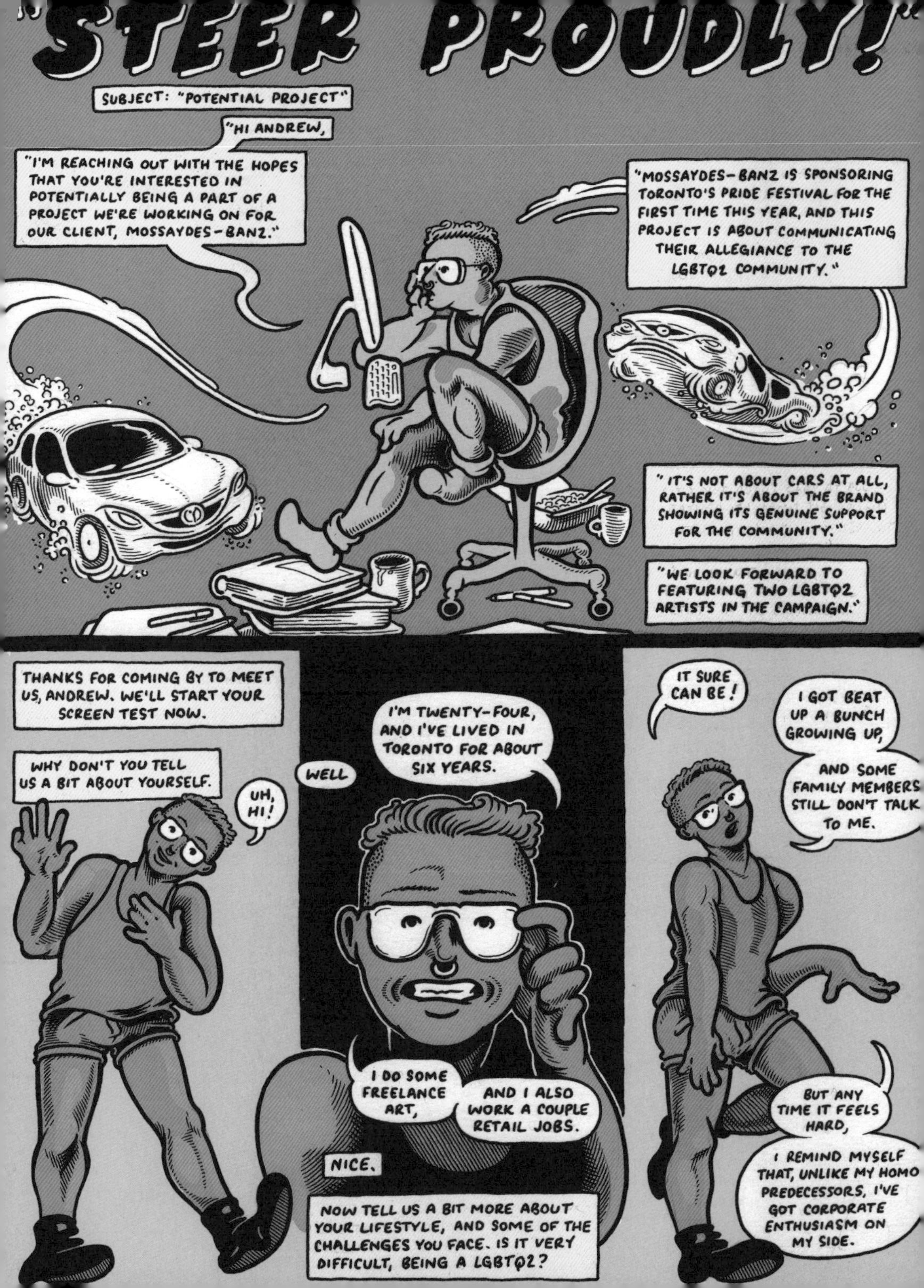
"STEER PROUDLY!"
SUBJECT: "POTENTIAL PROJECT"
"HI ANDREW,
"I'M REACHING OUT WITH THE HOPES THAT YOU'RE INTERESTED IN POTENTIALLY BEING A PART OF A PROJECT WE'RE WORKING ON FOR OUR CLIENT, MOSSAYDES-BANZ."
"MOSSAYDES-BANZ IS SPONSORING TORONTO'S PRIDE FESTIVAL FOR THE FIRST TIME THIS YEAR, AND THIS PROJECT IS ABOUT COMMUNICATING THEIR ALLEGIANCE TO THE LGBTQ2 COMMUNITY."
"IT'S NOT ABOUT CARS AT ALL, RATHER IT'S ABOUT THE BRAND SHOWING ITS GENUINE SUPPORT FOR THE COMMUNITY."
"WE LOOK FORWARD TO FEATURING TWO LGBTQ2 ARTISTS IN THE CAMPAIGN."
THANKS FOR COMING BY TO MEET US, ANDREW. WE'LL START YOUR SCREEN TEST NOW.
WHY DON'T YOU TELL US A BIT ABOUT YOURSELF.
UH, HI!
WELL
I'M TWENTY-FOUR, AND I'VE LIVED IN TORONTO FOR ABOUT SIX YEARS.
I DO SOME FREELANCE ART,
AND I ALSO WORK A COUPLE RETAIL JOBS.
NICE.
NOW TELL US A BIT MORE ABOUT YOUR LIFESTYLE, AND SOME OF THE CHALLENGES YOU FACE. IS IT VERY DIFFICULT, BEING A LGBTQ2?
IT SURE CAN BE!
I GOT BEAT UP A BUNCH GROWING UP,
AND SOME FAMILY MEMBERS STILL DON'T TALK TO ME.
BUT ANY TIME IT FEELS HARD,
I REMIND MYSELF THAT, UNLIKE MY HOMO PREDECESSORS, I'VE GOT CORPORATE ENTHUSIASM ON MY SIDE.

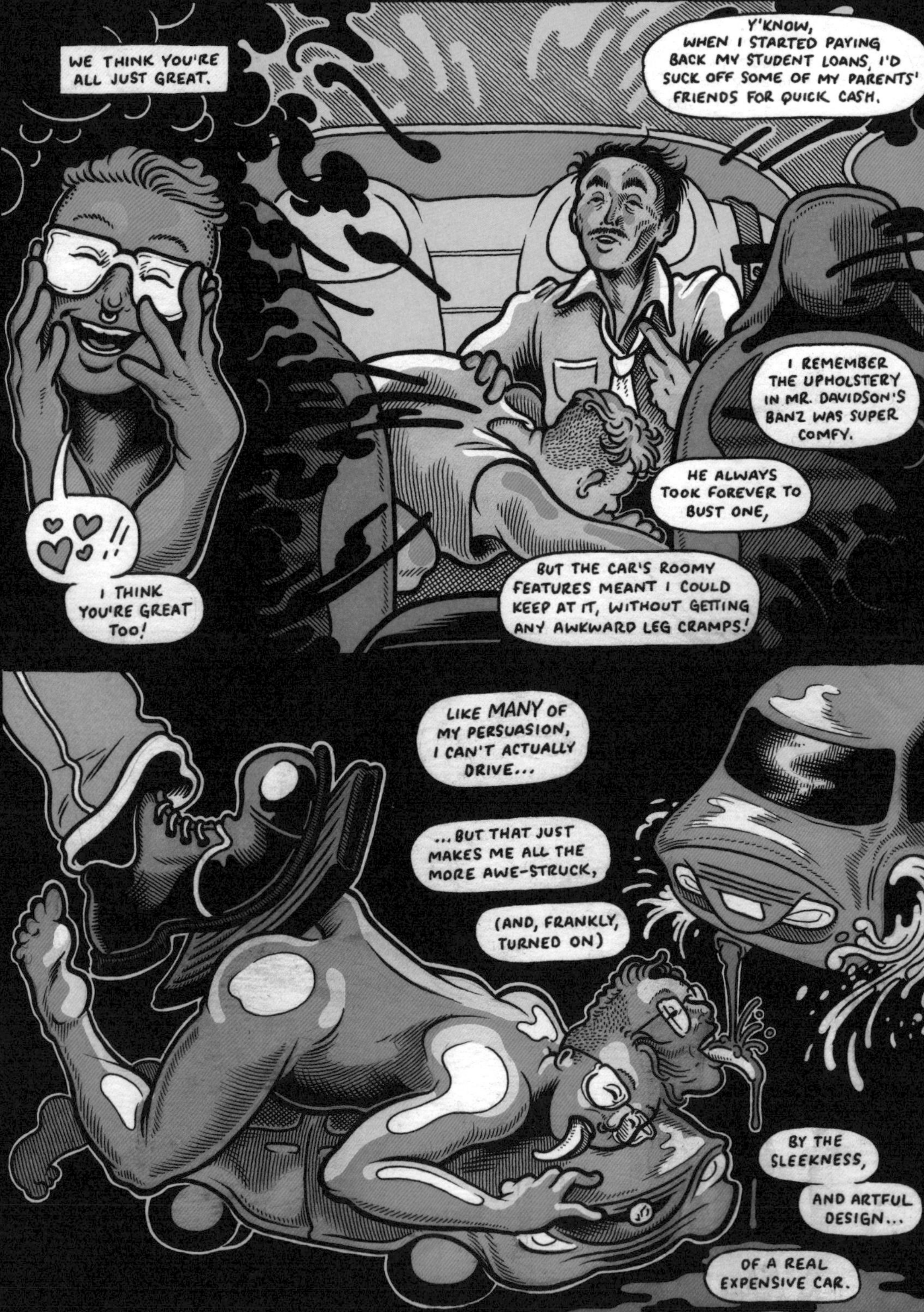
WE THINK YOU'RE ALL JUST GREAT.
!!
I THINK YOU'RE GREAT TOO!
Y'KNOW, WHEN I STARTED PAYING BACK MY STUDENT LOANS, I'D SUCK OFF SOME OF MY PARENTS' FRIENDS FOR QUICK CASH.
I REMEMBER THE UPHOLSTERY IN MR. DAVIDSON'S BANZ WAS SUPER COMFY.
HE ALWAYS TOOK FOREVER TO BUST ONE,
BUT THE CAR'S ROOMY FEATURES MEANT I COULD KEEP AT IT, WITHOUT GETTING ANY AWKWARD LEG CRAMPS!
LIKE MANY OF MY PERSUASION, I CAN'T ACTUALLY DRIVE...
...BUT THAT JUST MAKES ME ALL THE MORE AWE-STRUCK,
(AND, FRANKLY, TURNED ON)
BY THE SLEEKNESS,
AND ARTFUL DESIGN...
OF A REAL EXPENSIVE CAR.

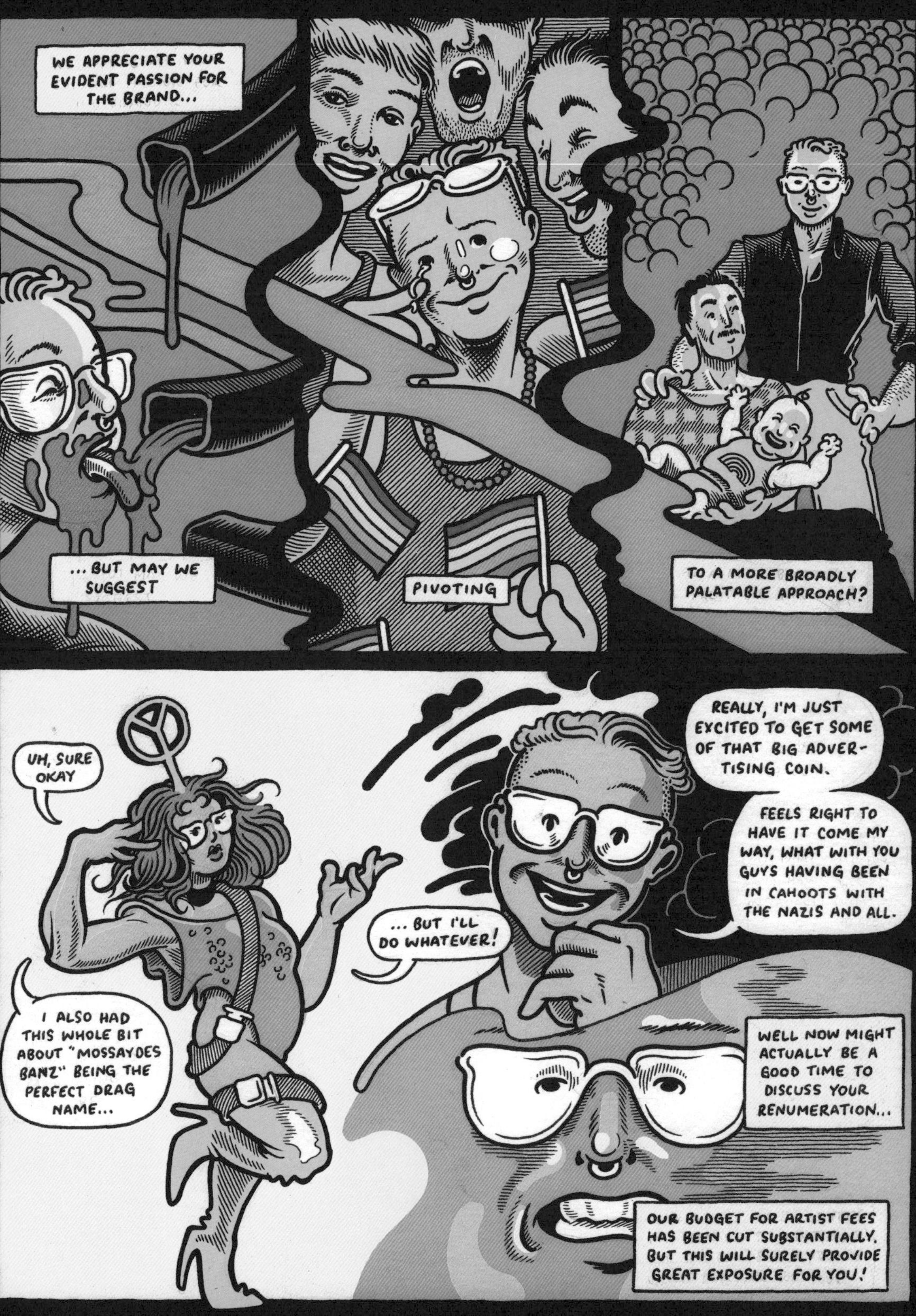
WE APPRECIATE YOUR EVIDENT PASSION FOR THE BRAND...
...BUT MAY WE SUGGEST
PIVOTING
TO A MORE BROADLY PALATABLE APPROACH?
UH, SURE OKAY
REALLY, I'M JUST EXCITED TO GET SOME OF THAT BIG ADVER-TISING COIN.
FEELS RIGHT TO HAVE IT COME MY WAY, WHAT WITH YOU GUYS HAVING BEEN IN CAHOOTS WITH THE NAZIS AND ALL.
...BUT I'LL DO WHATEVER!
I ALSO HAD THIS WHOLE BIT ABOUT "MOSSAYDES BANZ" BEING THE PERFECT DRAG NAME...
WELL NOW MIGHT ACTUALLY BE A GOOD TIME TO DISCUSS YOUR RENUMERATION...
OUR BUDGET FOR ARTIST FEES HAS BEEN CUT SUBSTANTIALLY. BUT THIS WILL SURELY PROVIDE GREAT EXPOSURE FOR YOU!

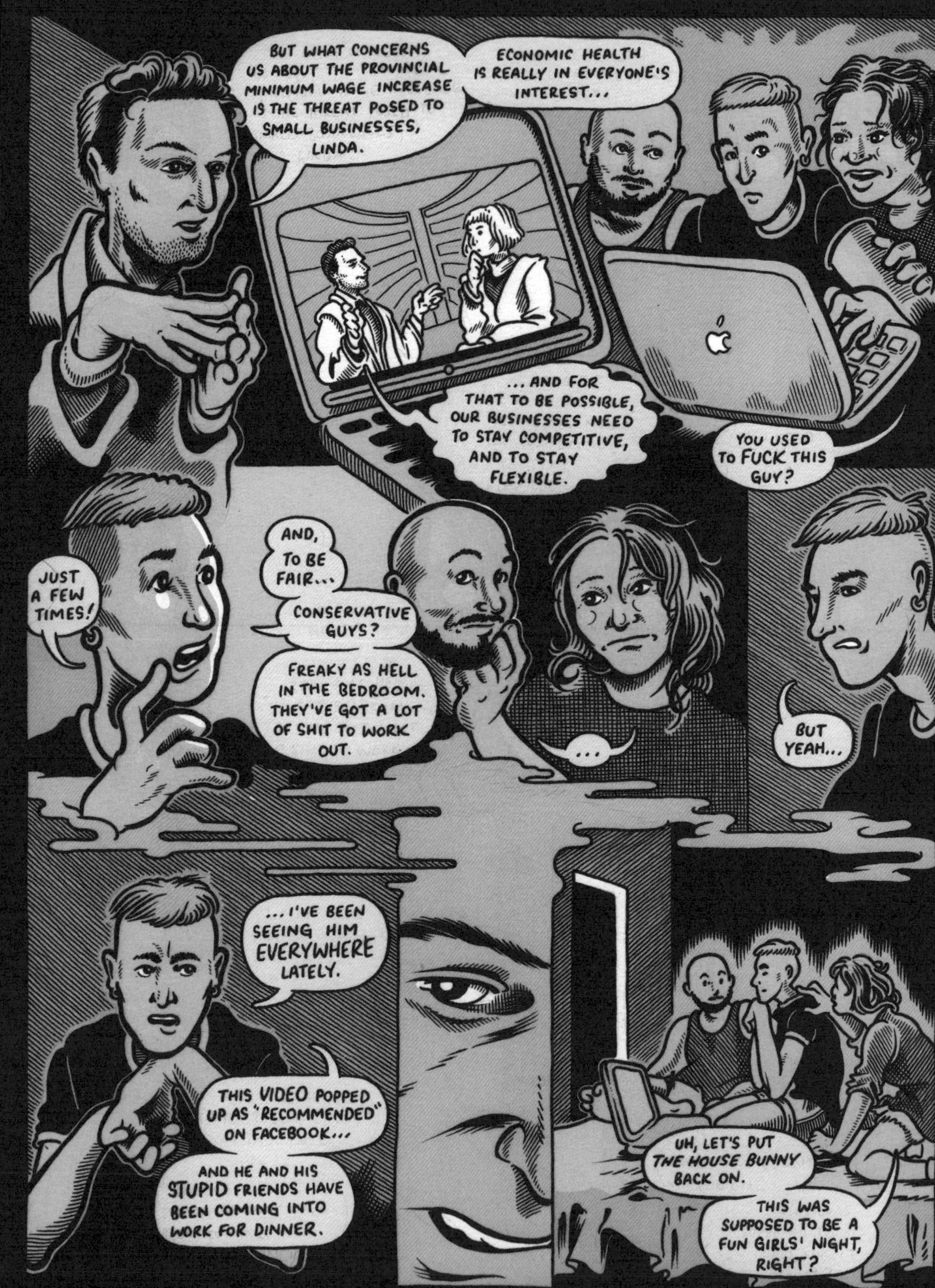
BUT WHAT CONCERNS US ABOUT THE PROVINCIAL MINIMUM WAGE INCREASE IS THE THREAT POSED TO SMALL BUSINESSES, LINDA.
ECONOMIC HEALTH IS REALLY IN EVERYONE'S INTEREST...
...AND FOR THAT TO BE POSSIBLE, OUR BUSINESSES NEED TO STAY COMPETITIVE, AND TO STAY FLEXIBLE.
YOU USED TO FUCK THIS GUY?
JUST A FEW TIMES!
AND, TO BE FAIR...
CONSERVATIVE GUYS?
FREAKY AS HELL IN THE BEDROOM. THEY'VE GOT A LOT OF SHIT TO WORK OUT.
...
BUT YEAH...
...I'VE BEEN SEEING HIM EVERYWHERE LATELY.
THIS VIDEO POPPED UP AS "RECOMMENDED" ON FACEBOOK...
AND HE AND HIS STUPID FRIENDS HAVE BEEN COMING INTO WORK FOR DINNER.
UH, LET'S PUT THE HOUSE BUNNY BACK ON.
THIS WAS SUPPOSED TO BE A FUN GIRLS' NIGHT, RIGHT?

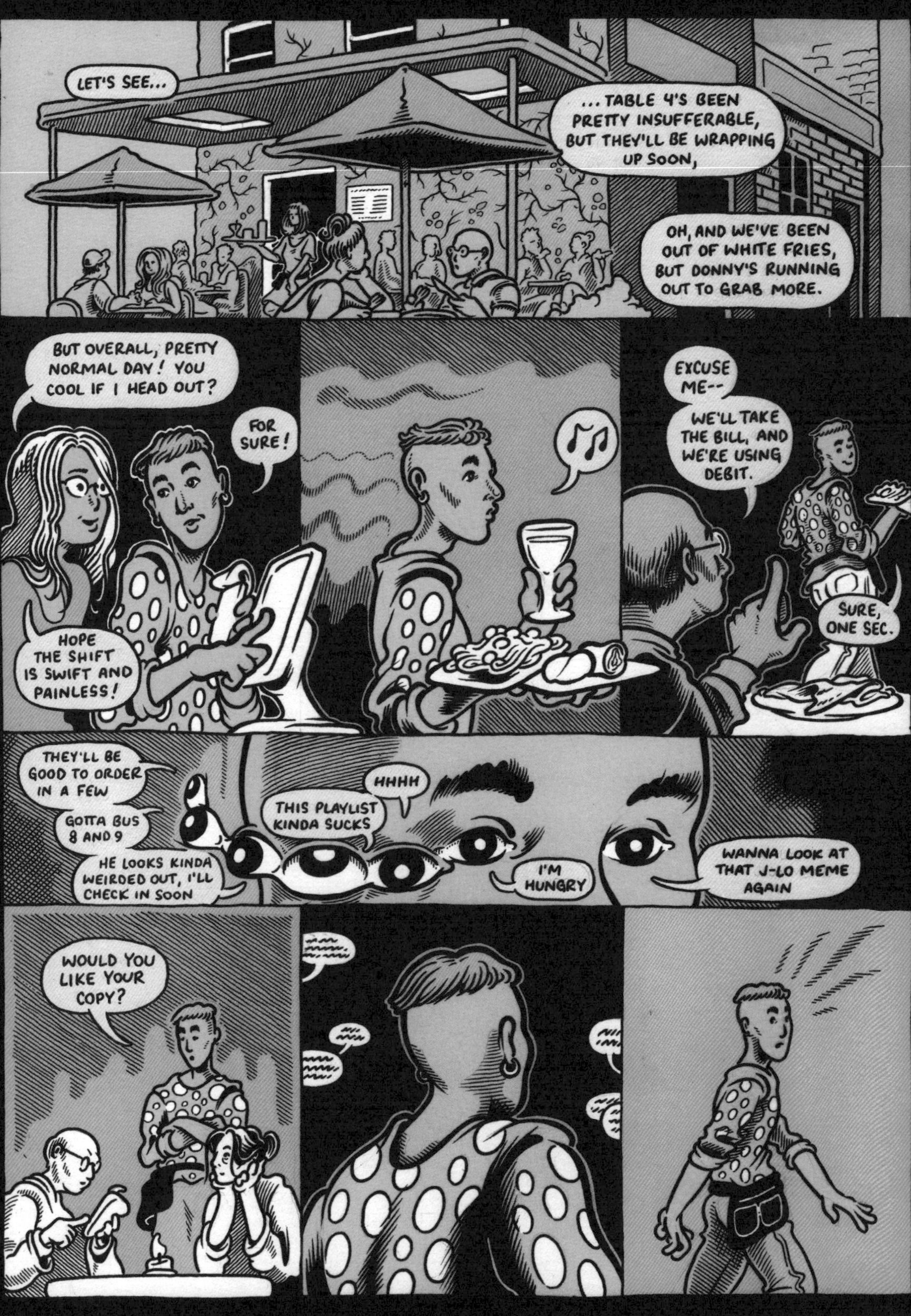
LET'S SEE...
...TABLE 4'S BEEN PRETTY INSUFFERABLE, BUT THEY'LL BE WRAPPING UP SOON,
OH, AND WE'VE BEEN OUT OF WHITE FRIES, BUT DONNY'S RUNNING OUT TO GRAB MORE.
BUT OVERALL, PRETTY NORMAL DAY! YOU COOL IF I HEAD OUT?
FOR SURE!
HOPE THE SHIFT IS SWIFT AND PAINLESS!
♪♫
EXCUSE ME--
WE'LL TAKE THE BILL, AND WE'RE USING DEBIT.
SURE, ONE SEC.
THEY'LL BE GOOD TO ORDER IN A FEW
GOTTA BUS 8 AND 9
HE LOOKS KINDA WEIRDED OUT, I'LL CHECK IN SOON
HHHH
THIS PLAYLIST KINDA SUCKS
I'M HUNGRY
WANNA LOOK AT THAT J-LO MEME AGAIN
WOULD YOU LIKE YOUR COPY?

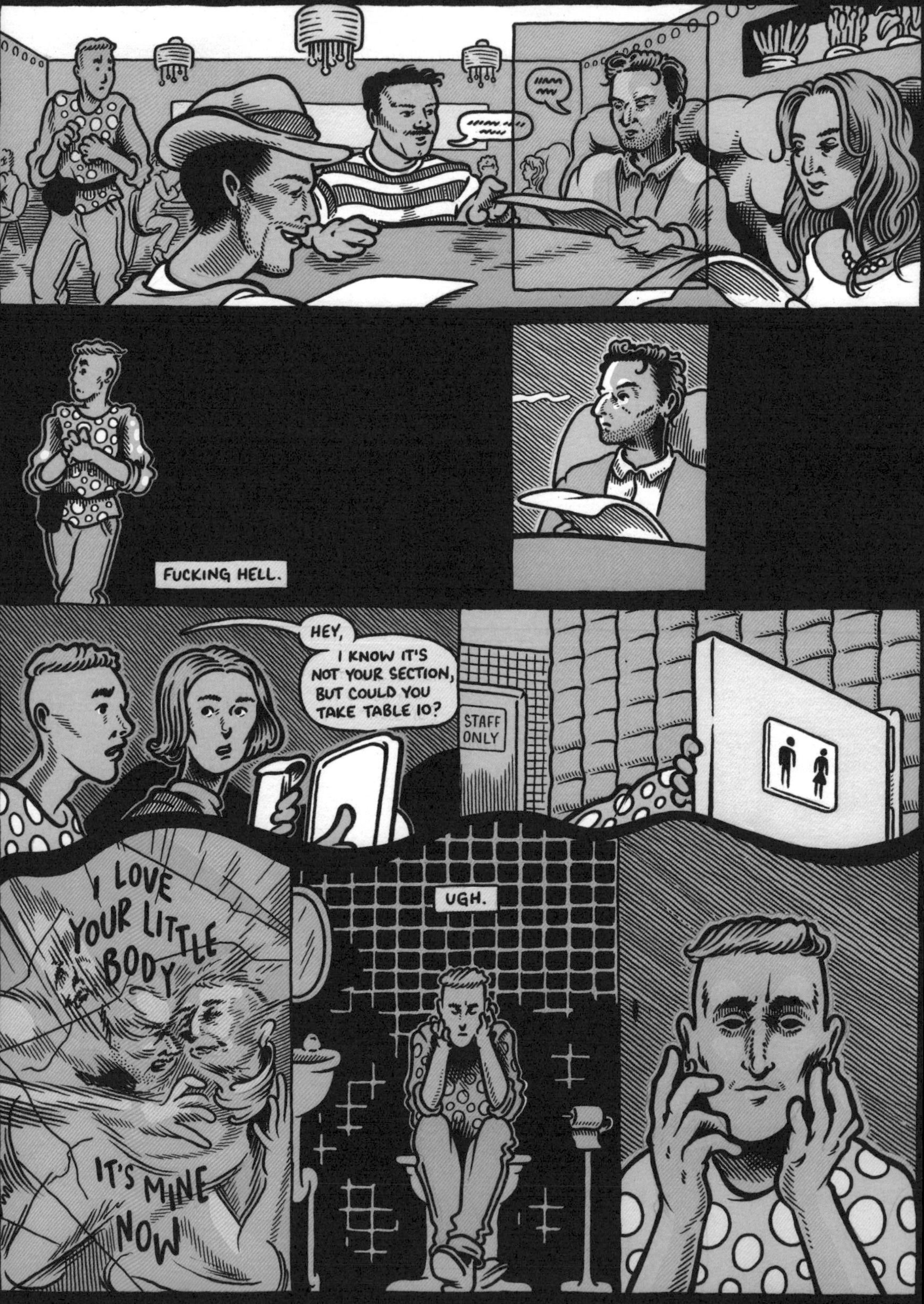
FUCKING HELL.
HEY, I KNOW IT'S NOT YOUR SECTION, BUT COULD YOU TAKE TABLE 10?
STAFF ONLY
I LOVE YOUR LITTLE BODY
IT'S MINE NOW
UGH.

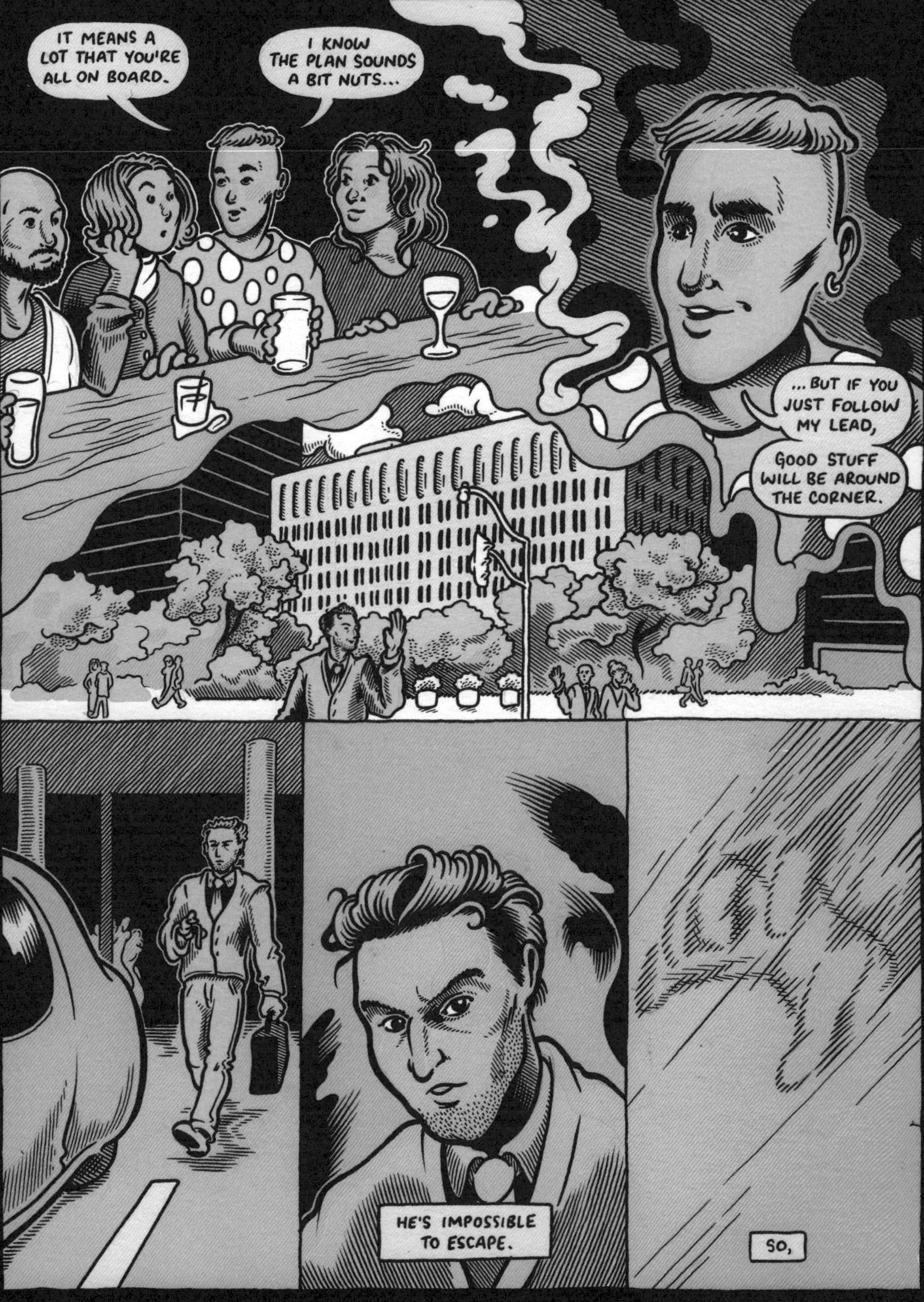
IT MEANS A LOT THAT YOU'RE ALL ON BOARD.
I KNOW THE PLAN SOUNDS A BIT NUTS...
... BUT IF YOU JUST FOLLOW MY LEAD,
GOOD STUFF WILL BE AROUND THE CORNER.
HE'S IMPOSSIBLE TO ESCAPE.
SO,

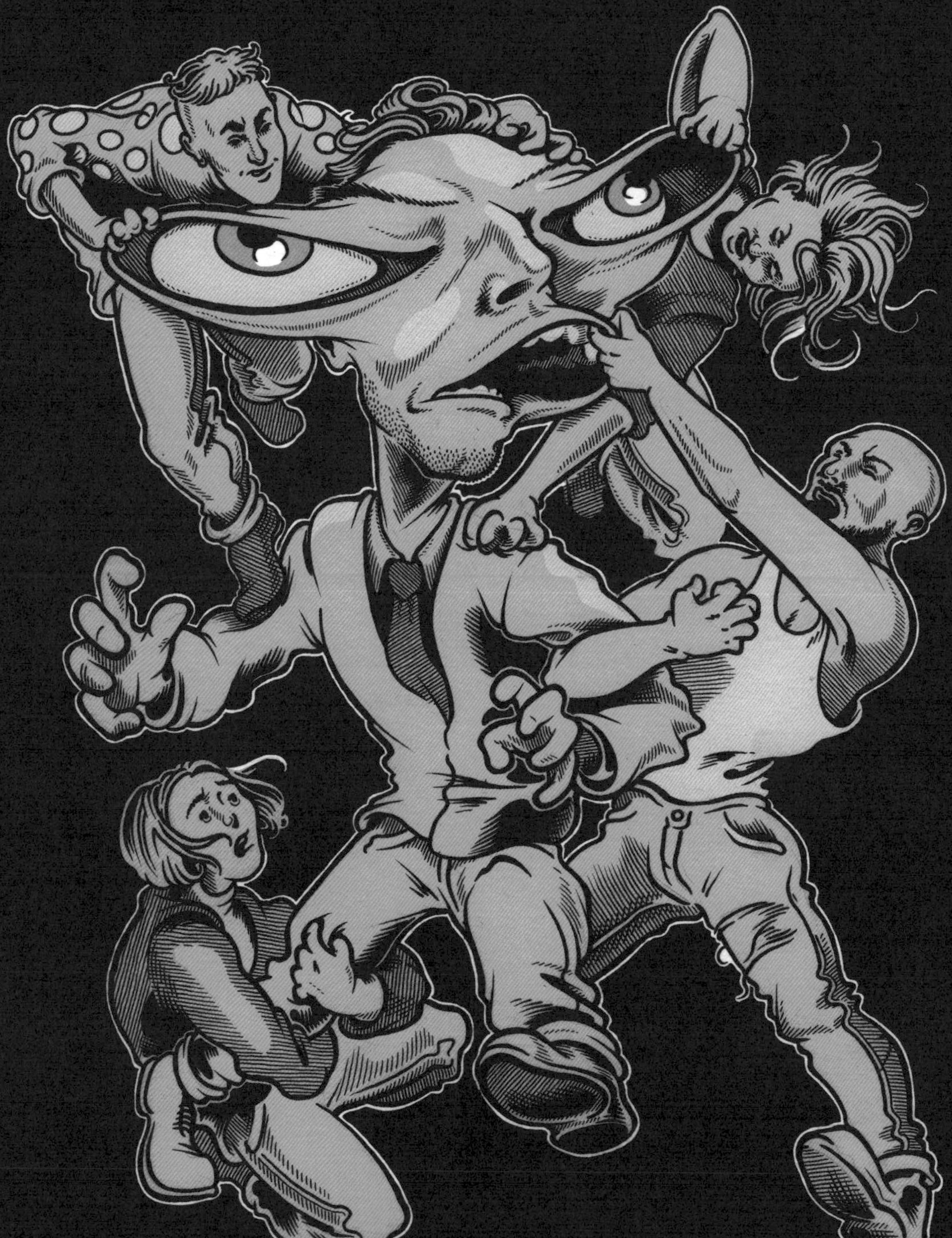

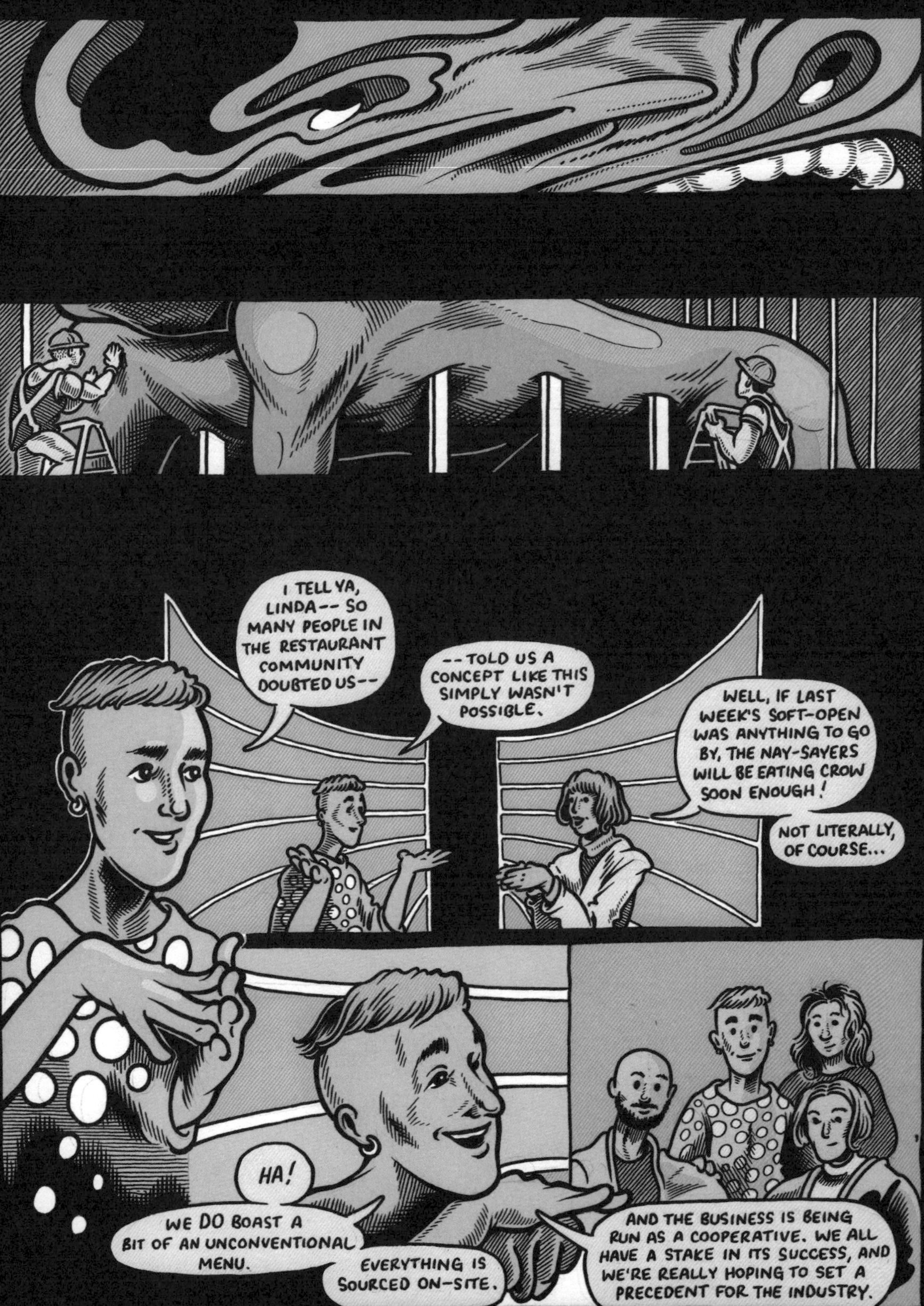
I TELL YA, LINDA-- SO MANY PEOPLE IN THE RESTAURANT COMMUNITY DOUBTED US--
--TOLD US A CONCEPT LIKE THIS SIMPLY WASN'T POSSIBLE.
WELL, IF LAST WEEK'S SOFT-OPEN WAS ANYTHING TO GO BY, THE NAY-SAYERS WILL BE EATING CROW SOON ENOUGH!
NOT LITERALLY, OF COURSE...
HA!
WE DO BOAST A BIT OF AN UNCONVENTIONAL MENU.
EVERYTHING IS SOURCED ON-SITE.
AND THE BUSINESS IS BEING RUN AS A COOPERATIVE. WE ALL HAVE A STAKE IN ITS SUCCESS, AND WE'RE REALLY HOPING TO SET A PRECEDENT FOR THE INDUSTRY.

GRAND OPENING!

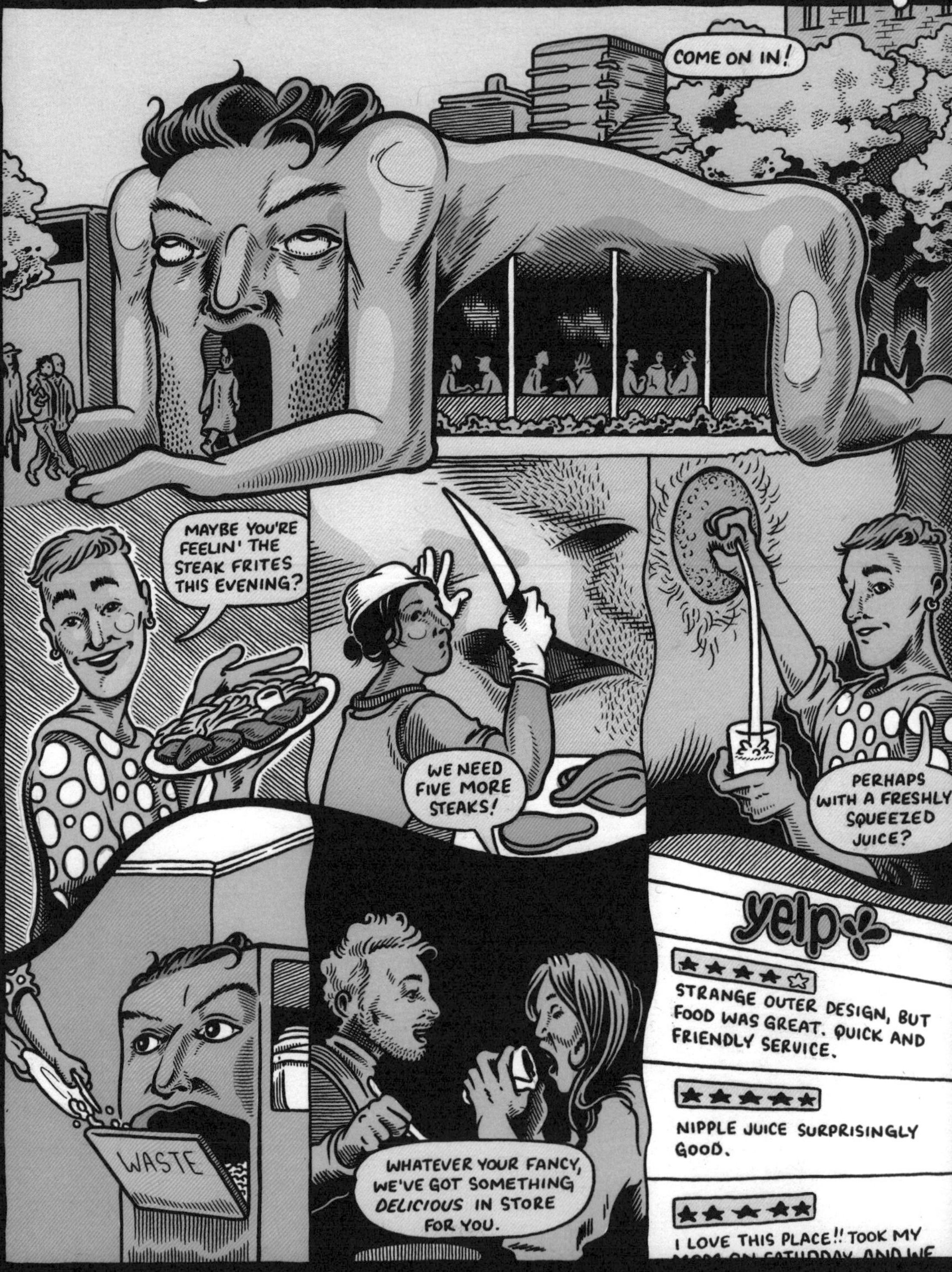
COME ON IN!
MAYBE YOU'RE FEELIN' THE STEAK FRITES THIS EVENING?
WE NEED FIVE MORE STEAKS!
PERHAPS WITH A FRESHLY SQUEEZED JUICE?
WASTE
WHATEVER YOUR FANCY, WE'VE GOT SOMETHING *DELICIOUS* IN STORE FOR YOU.
yelp
STRANGE OUTER DESIGN, BUT FOOD WAS GREAT. QUICK AND FRIENDLY SERVICE.
NIPPLE JUICE SURPRISINGLY GOOD.
I LOVE THIS PLACE!! TOOK MY

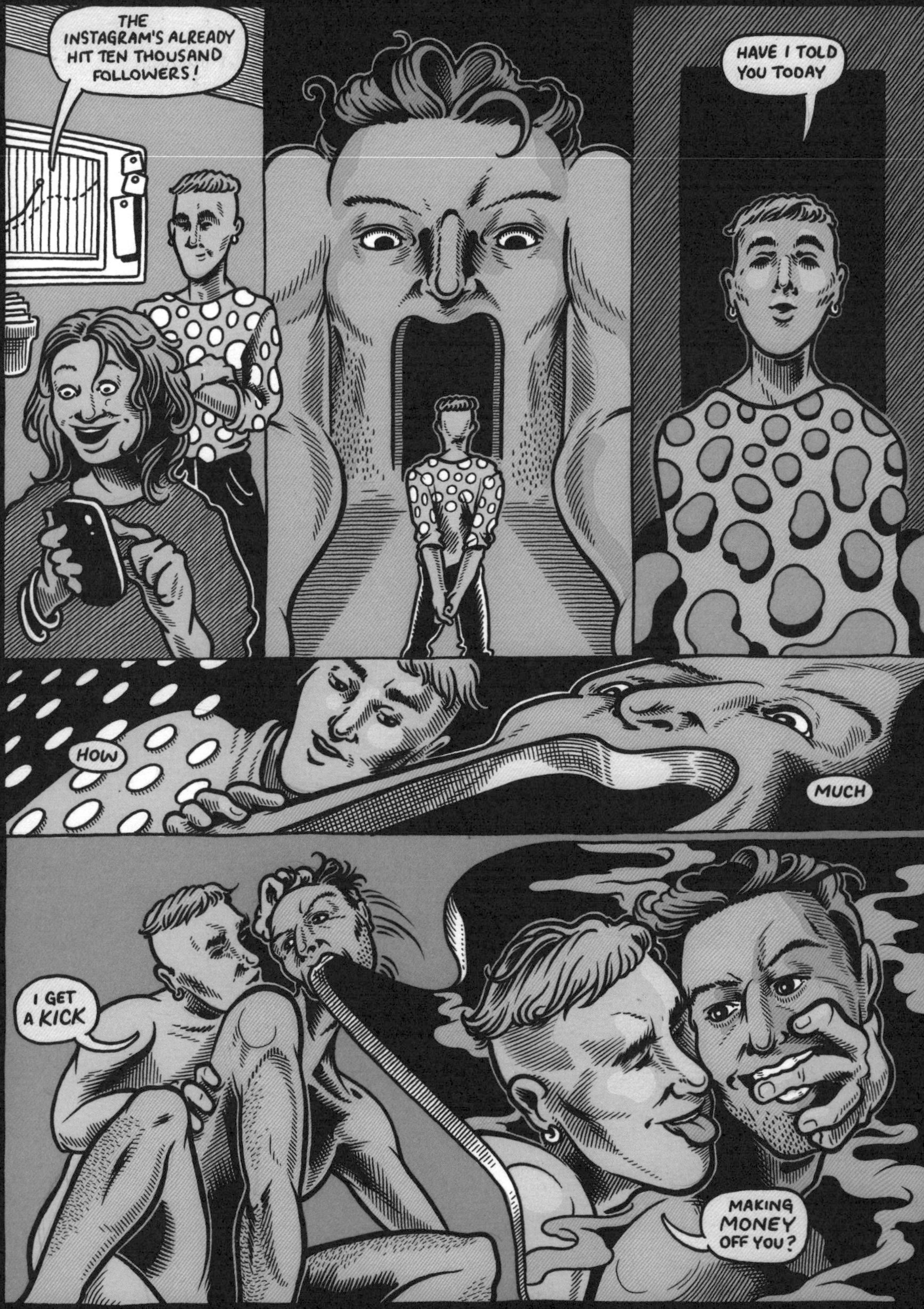
THE INSTAGRAM'S ALREADY HIT TEN THOUSAND FOLLOWERS!
HAVE I TOLD YOU TODAY
HOW
MUCH
I GET A KICK
MAKING MONEY OFF YOU?

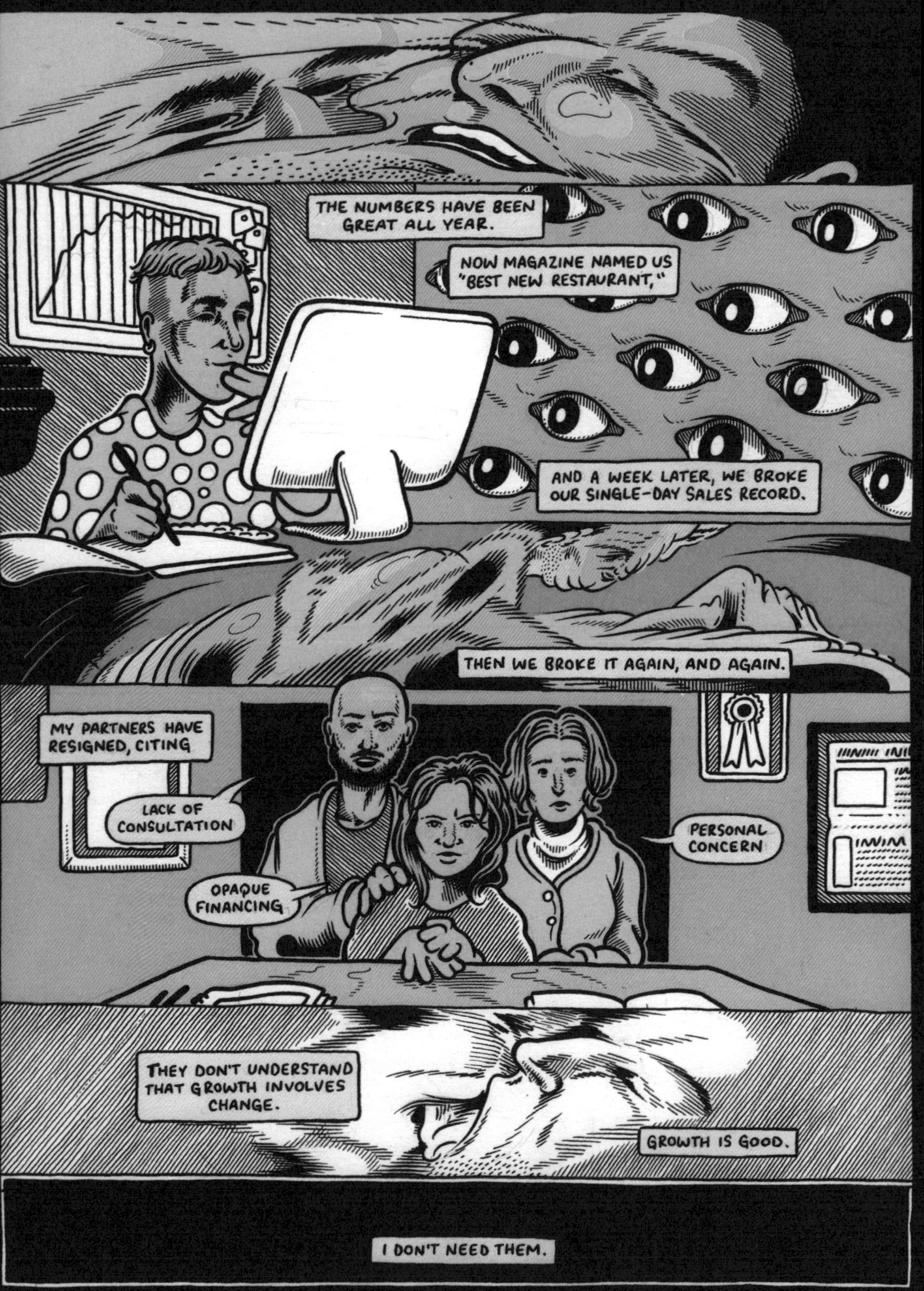

THE NUMBERS HAVE BEEN GREAT ALL YEAR.
NOW MAGAZINE NAMED US "BEST NEW RESTAURANT,"
AND A WEEK LATER, WE BROKE OUR SINGLE-DAY SALES RECORD.
THEN WE BROKE IT AGAIN, AND AGAIN.
MY PARTNERS HAVE RESIGNED, CITING
LACK OF CONSULTATION
OPAQUE FINANCING
PERSONAL CONCERN
THEY DON'T UNDERSTAND THAT GROWTH INVOLVES CHANGE.
GROWTH IS GOOD.
I DON'T NEED THEM.

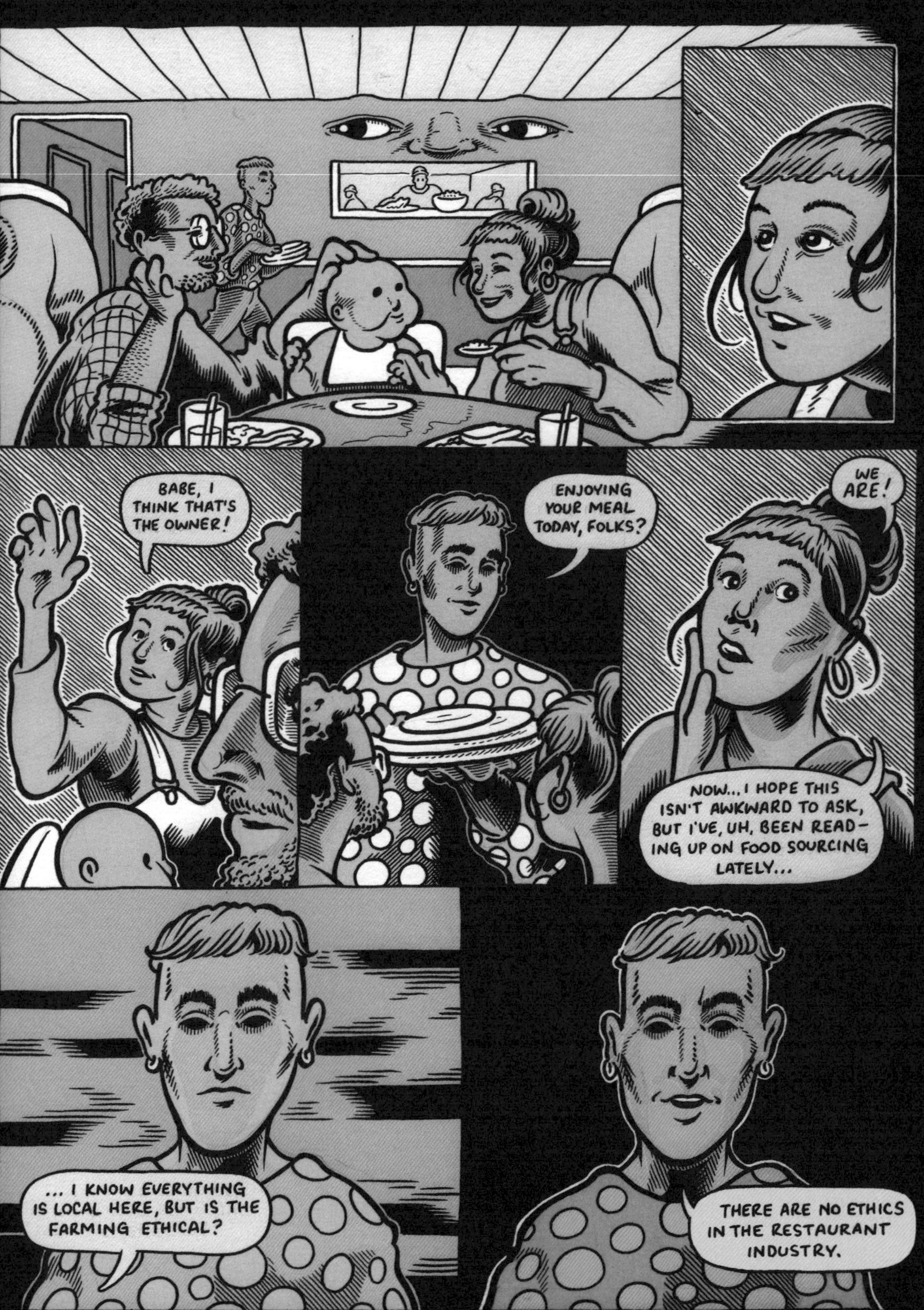
BABE, I THINK THAT'S THE OWNER!
ENJOYING YOUR MEAL TODAY, FOLKS?
WE ARE!
NOW... I HOPE THIS ISN'T AWKWARD TO ASK, BUT I'VE, UH, BEEN READING UP ON FOOD SOURCING LATELY...
... I KNOW EVERYTHING IS LOCAL HERE, BUT IS THE FARMING ETHICAL?
THERE ARE NO ETHICS IN THE RESTAURANT INDUSTRY.

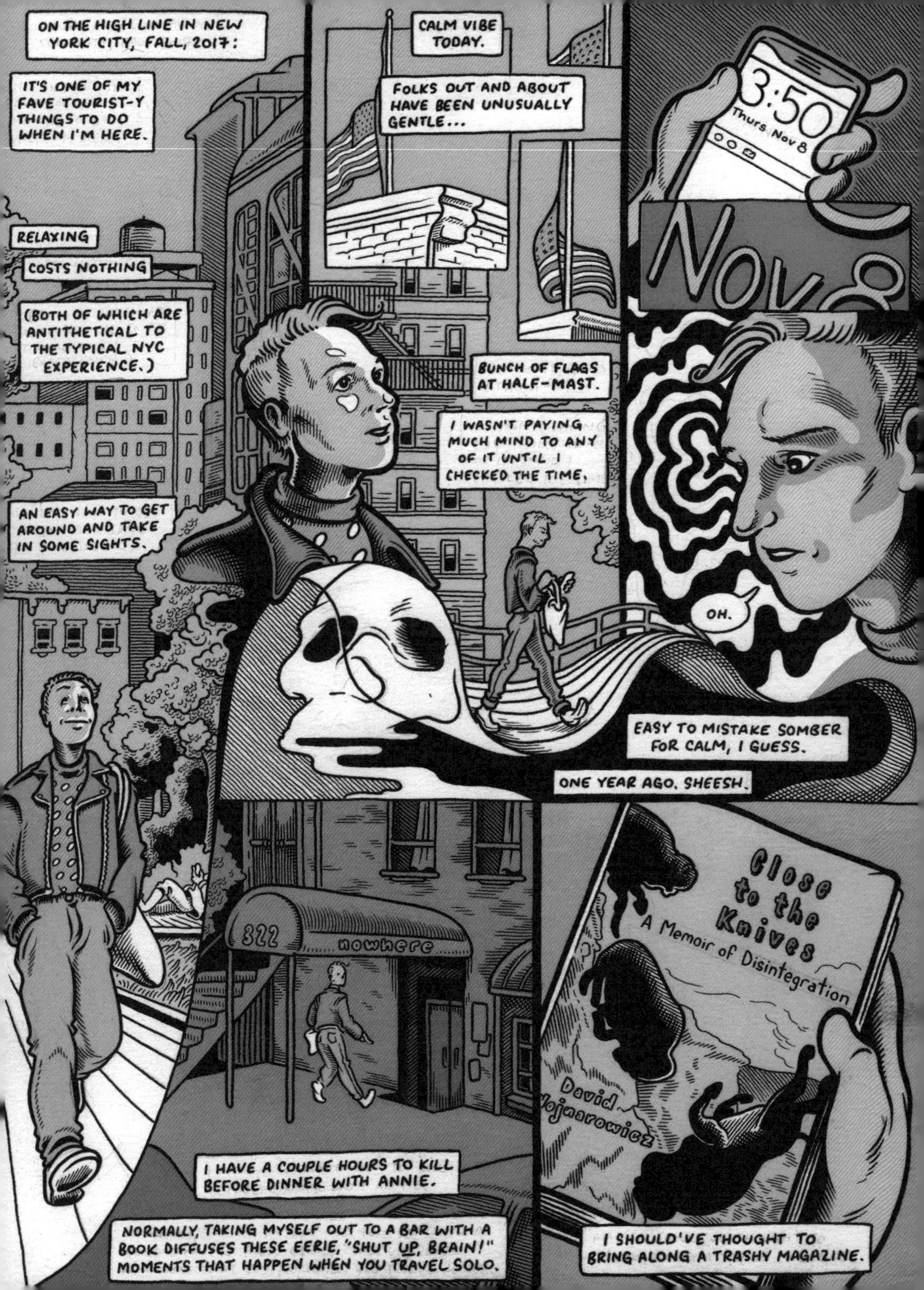

ON THE HIGH LINE IN NEW YORK CITY, FALL, 2017:
IT'S ONE OF MY FAVE TOURIST-Y THINGS TO DO WHEN I'M HERE.
RELAXING
COSTS NOTHING
(BOTH OF WHICH ARE ANTITHETICAL TO THE TYPICAL NYC EXPERIENCE.)
AN EASY WAY TO GET AROUND AND TAKE IN SOME SIGHTS.
CALM VIBE TODAY.
FOLKS OUT AND ABOUT HAVE BEEN UNUSUALLY GENTLE...
BUNCH OF FLAGS AT HALF-MAST.
I WASN'T PAYING MUCH MIND TO ANY OF IT UNTIL I CHECKED THE TIME.
3:50
Thurs Nov 8
Nov 8
OH.
EASY TO MISTAKE SOMBER FOR CALM, I GUESS.
ONE YEAR AGO. SHEESH.
322
nowhere
I HAVE A COUPLE HOURS TO KILL BEFORE DINNER WITH ANNIE.
NORMALLY, TAKING MYSELF OUT TO A BAR WITH A BOOK DIFFUSES THESE EERIE, "SHUT UP, BRAIN!" MOMENTS THAT HAPPEN WHEN YOU TRAVEL SOLO.
Close to the Knives
A Memoir of Disintegration
David Wojnarowicz
I SHOULD'VE THOUGHT TO BRING ALONG A TRASHY MAGAZINE.

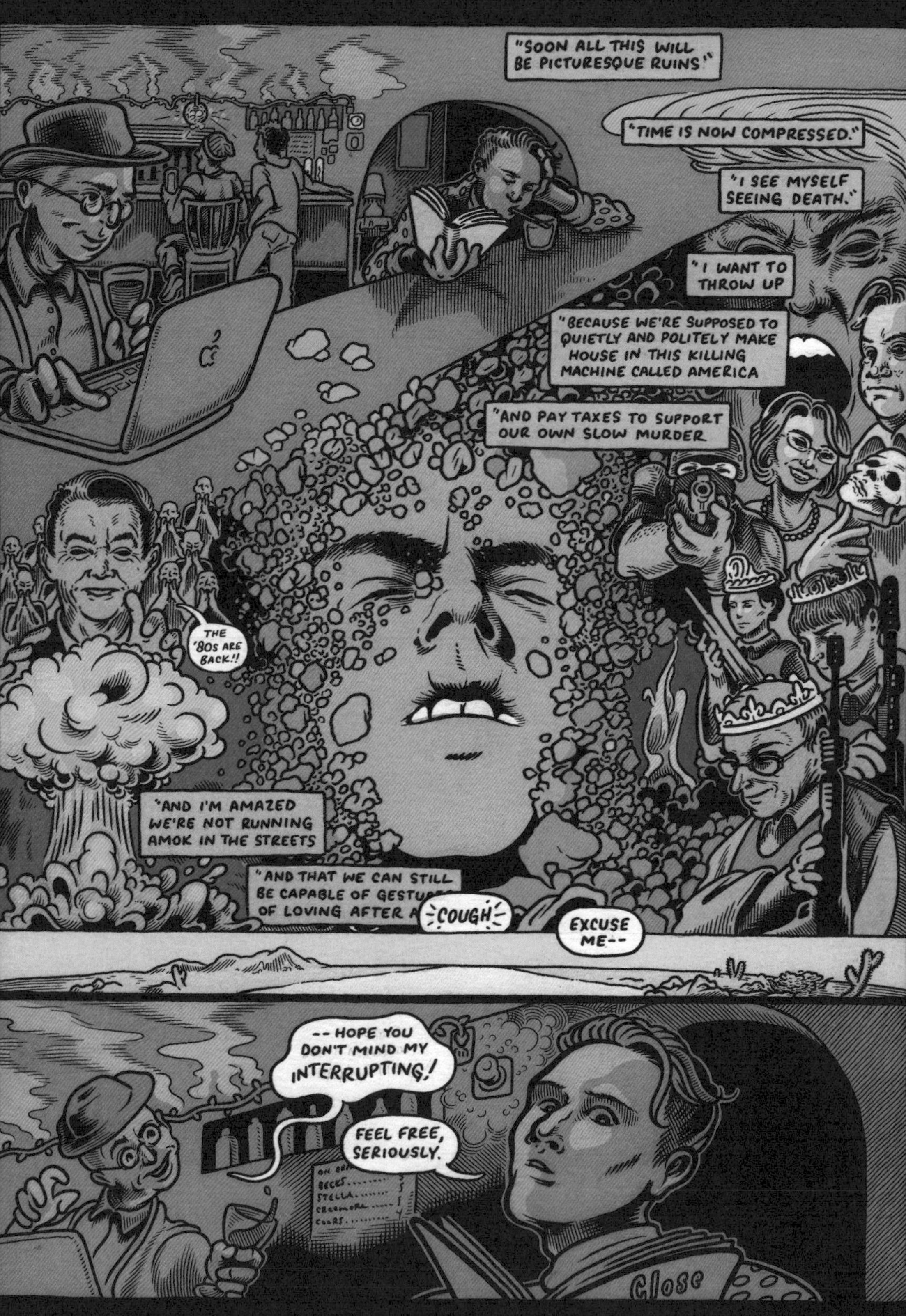
"SOON ALL THIS WILL BE PICTURESQUE RUINS."
"TIME IS NOW COMPRESSED."
"I SEE MYSELF SEEING DEATH."
"I WANT TO THROW UP
"BECAUSE WE'RE SUPPOSED TO QUIETLY AND POLITELY MAKE HOUSE IN THIS KILLING MACHINE CALLED AMERICA
"AND PAY TAXES TO SUPPORT OUR OWN SLOW MURDER
THE '80S ARE BACK!!
"AND I'M AMAZED WE'RE NOT RUNNING AMOK IN THE STREETS
"AND THAT WE CAN STILL BE CAPABLE OF GESTUR
OF LOVING AFTER A
COUGH!
EXCUSE ME--
--HOPE YOU DON'T MIND MY INTERRUPTING!
FEEL FREE, SERIOUSLY.
Close

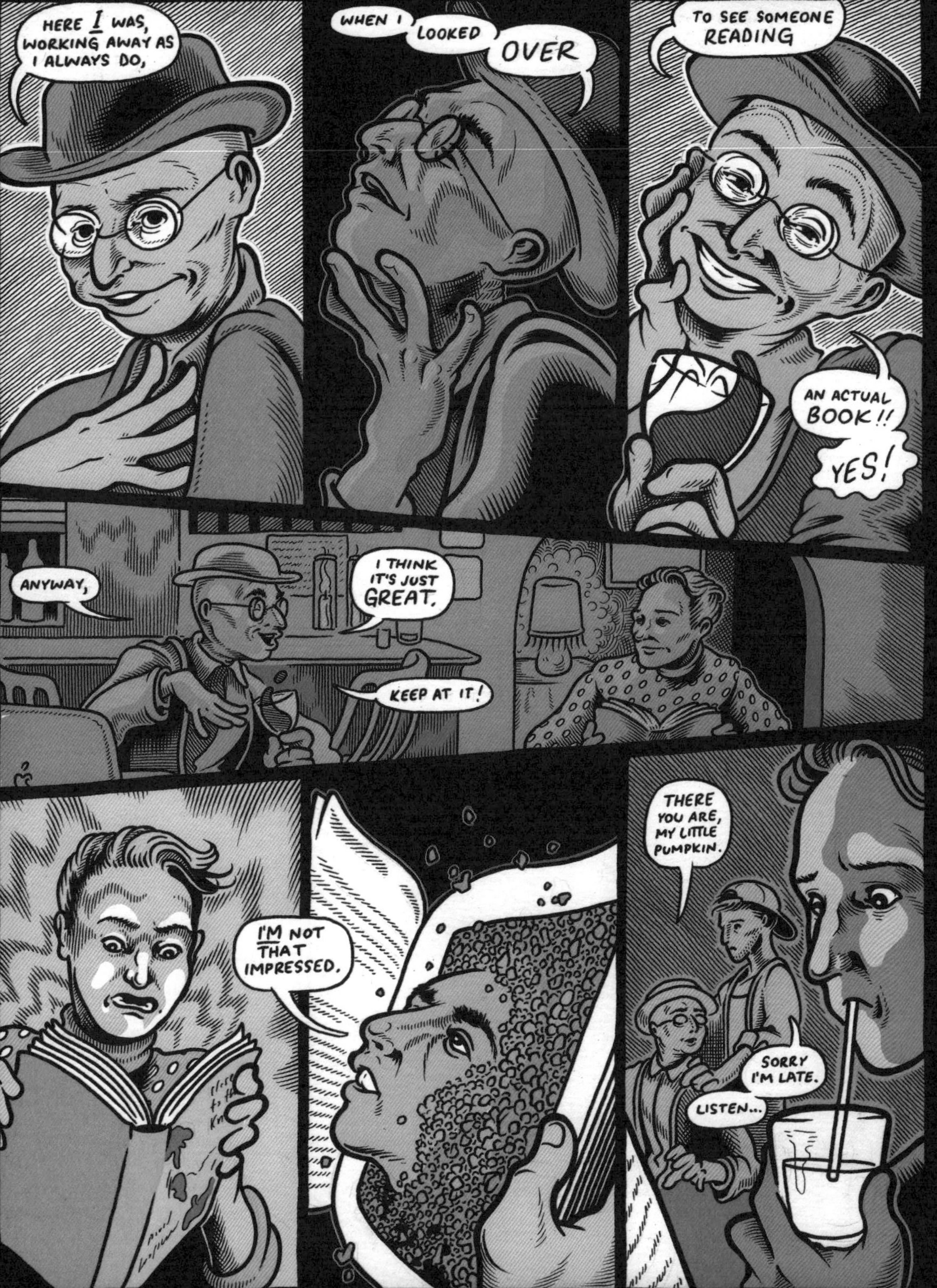
HERE I WAS, WORKING AWAY AS I ALWAYS DO,
WHEN I
LOOKED
OVER
TO SEE SOMEONE READING
AN ACTUAL BOOK!!
YES!
ANYWAY,
I THINK IT'S JUST GREAT.
KEEP AT IT!
I'M NOT THAT IMPRESSED.
THERE YOU ARE, MY LITTLE PUMPKIN.
SORRY I'M LATE.
LISTEN...

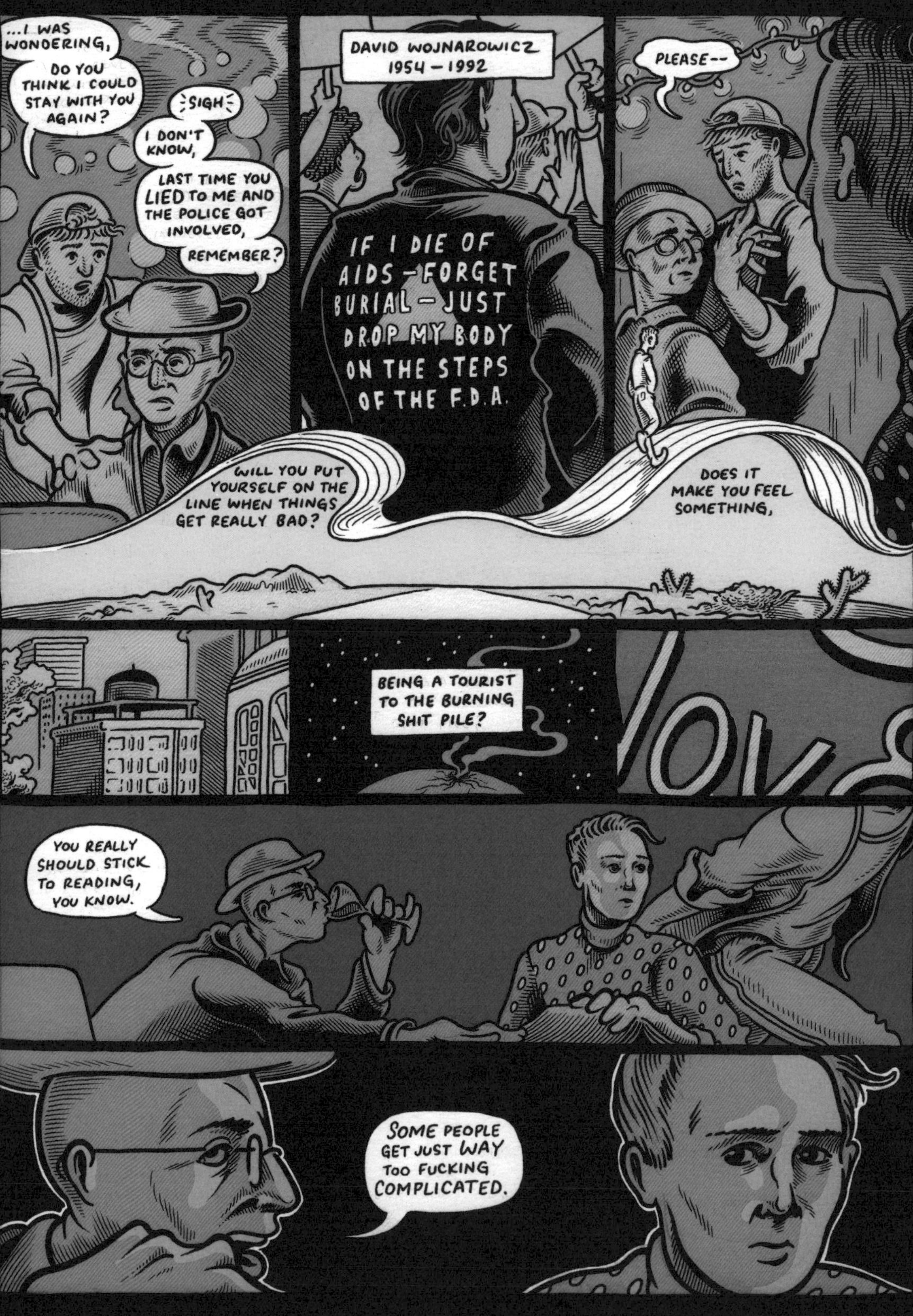

...I WAS WONDERING,
DO YOU THINK I COULD STAY WITH YOU AGAIN?
SIGH
I DON'T KNOW,
LAST TIME YOU LIED TO ME AND THE POLICE GOT INVOLVED,
REMEMBER?
DAVID WOJNAROWICZ 1954 – 1992
IF I DIE OF AIDS – FORGET BURIAL – JUST DROP MY BODY ON THE STEPS OF THE F.D.A.
PLEASE--
WILL YOU PUT YOURSELF ON THE LINE WHEN THINGS GET REALLY BAD?
DOES IT MAKE YOU FEEL SOMETHING,
BEING A TOURIST TO THE BURNING SHIT PILE?
YOU REALLY SHOULD STICK TO READING, YOU KNOW.
SOME PEOPLE GET JUST WAY TOO FUCKING COMPLICATED.

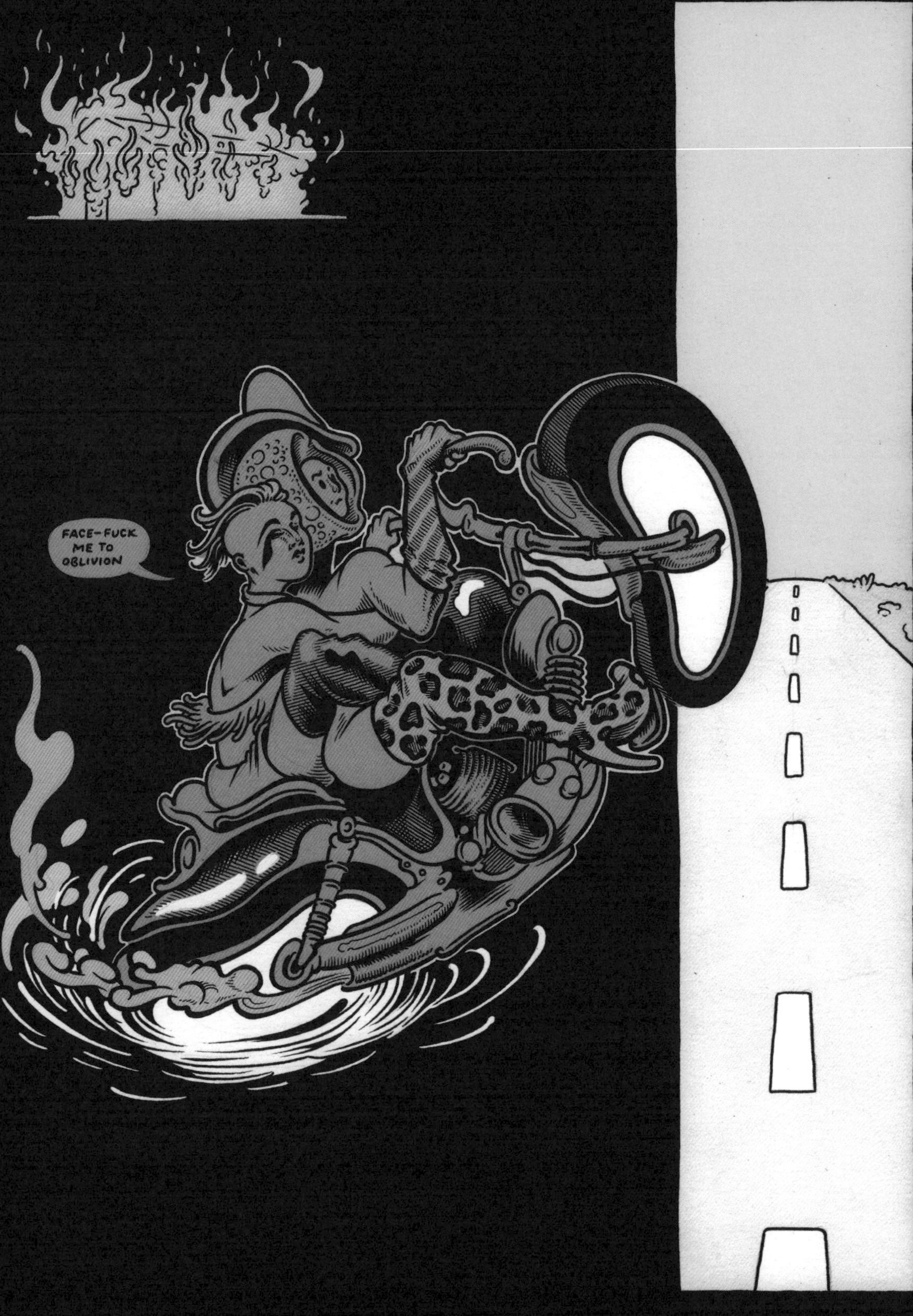
FACE-FUCK ME TO OBLIVION

ASSEMBLY
ALL THE BAD NEWS HAD BACKED ME INTO A CORNER, INTO THIS REALLY DREADFUL INERTIA.
I'D BEEN STAYING IN FOR MONTHS ON END. GOTTA SAVE SOME MONEY, GOTTA KEEP MY HEAD DOWN.
GET IT TOGETHER!
GET IT TOGETHER!
I'D BEEN PORING OVER SOME SCALDING-HOT TAKES
MY HANDS DRIFTED
AND BEFORE I KNEW IT, THEY WERE PUTTING MY FACE ON.
LIKE, UGH
WHAT
WHYYY
EVERYTHING'S CRUMBLING
I'M PUTTING MY COAT ON.
GET
IT
TOGETHER!
THE COLD EVENING AIR IS A PUNCH IN THE FACE, EUCH--
--BUT I'M DOIN' IT.
HAPPY?

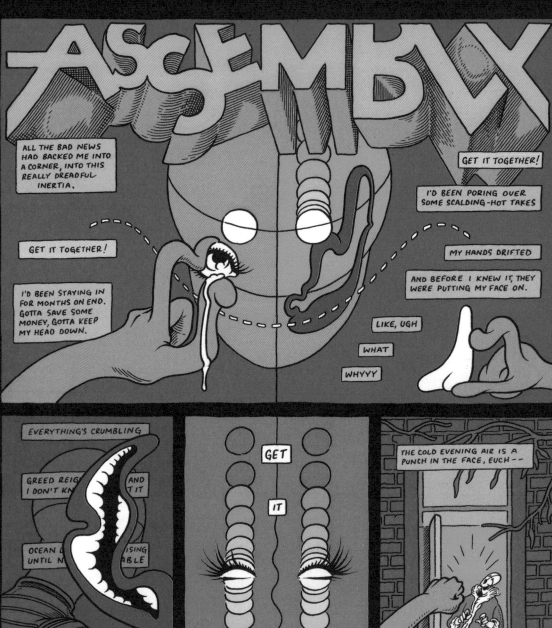

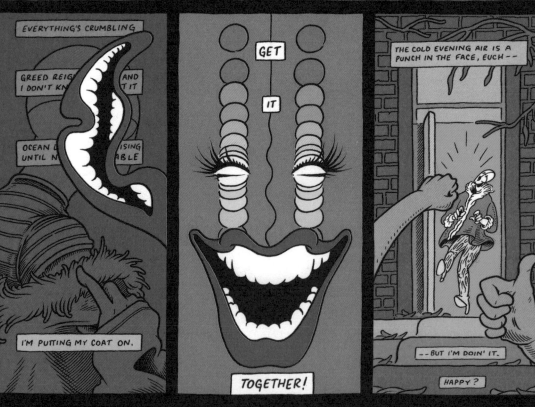

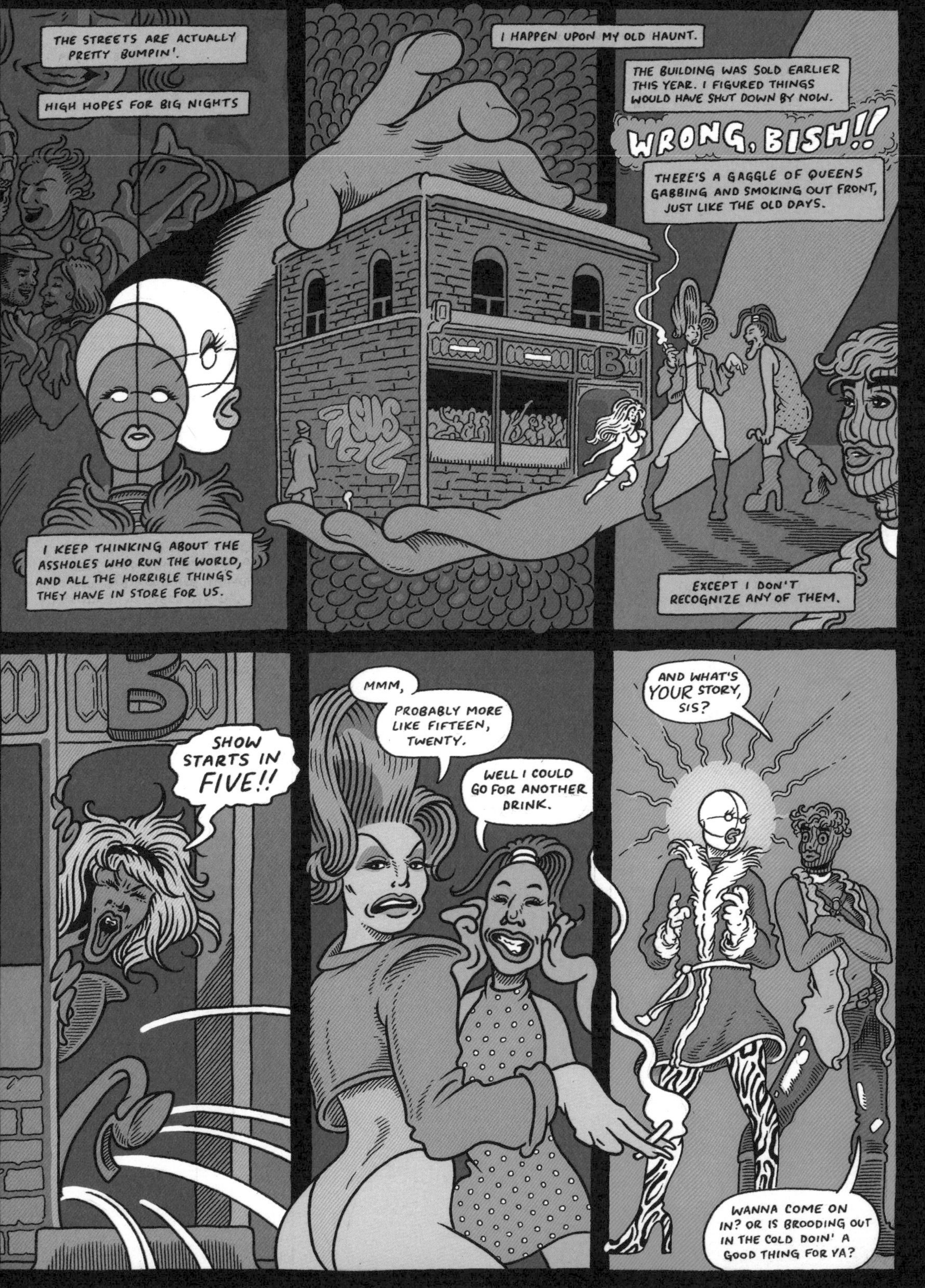

THE STREETS ARE ACTUALLY PRETTY BUMPIN'.
HIGH HOPES FOR BIG NIGHTS
I KEEP THINKING ABOUT THE ASSHOLES WHO RUN THE WORLD, AND ALL THE HORRIBLE THINGS THEY HAVE IN STORE FOR US.
I HAPPEN UPON MY OLD HAUNT.
THE BUILDING WAS SOLD EARLIER THIS YEAR. I FIGURED THINGS WOULD HAVE SHUT DOWN BY NOW.
WRONG, BISH!!
THERE'S A GAGGLE OF QUEENS GABBING AND SMOKING OUT FRONT, JUST LIKE THE OLD DAYS.
EXCEPT I DON'T RECOGNIZE ANY OF THEM.
SHOW STARTS IN FIVE!!
MMM,
PROBABLY MORE LIKE FIFTEEN, TWENTY.
WELL I COULD GO FOR ANOTHER DRINK.
AND WHAT'S YOUR STORY, SIS?
WANNA COME ON IN? OR IS BROODING OUT IN THE COLD DOIN' A GOOD THING FOR YA?

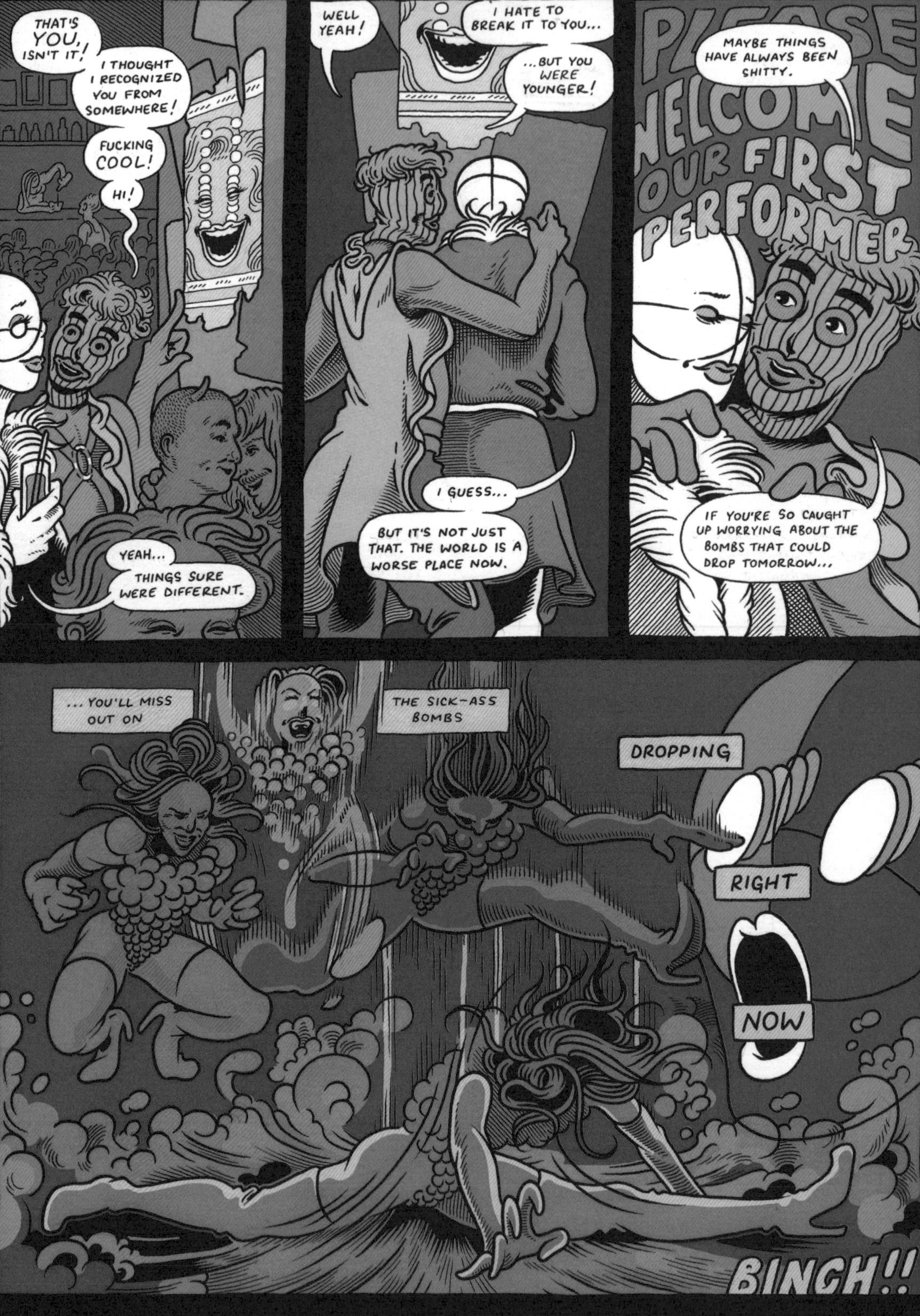

THAT'S YOU, ISN'T IT?
I THOUGHT I RECOGNIZED YOU FROM SOMEWHERE!
FUCKING COOL!
HI!
YEAH...
THINGS SURE WERE DIFFERENT.
WELL YEAH!
I HATE TO BREAK IT TO YOU...
...BUT YOU WERE YOUNGER!
I GUESS...
BUT IT'S NOT JUST THAT. THE WORLD IS A WORSE PLACE NOW.
PLEASE WELCOME OUR FIRST PERFORMER
MAYBE THINGS HAVE ALWAYS BEEN SHITTY.
IF YOU'RE SO CAUGHT UP WORRYING ABOUT THE BOMBS THAT COULD DROP TOMORROW...
...YOU'LL MISS OUT ON
THE SICK-ASS BOMBS
DROPPING
RIGHT
NOW
BINGH!!

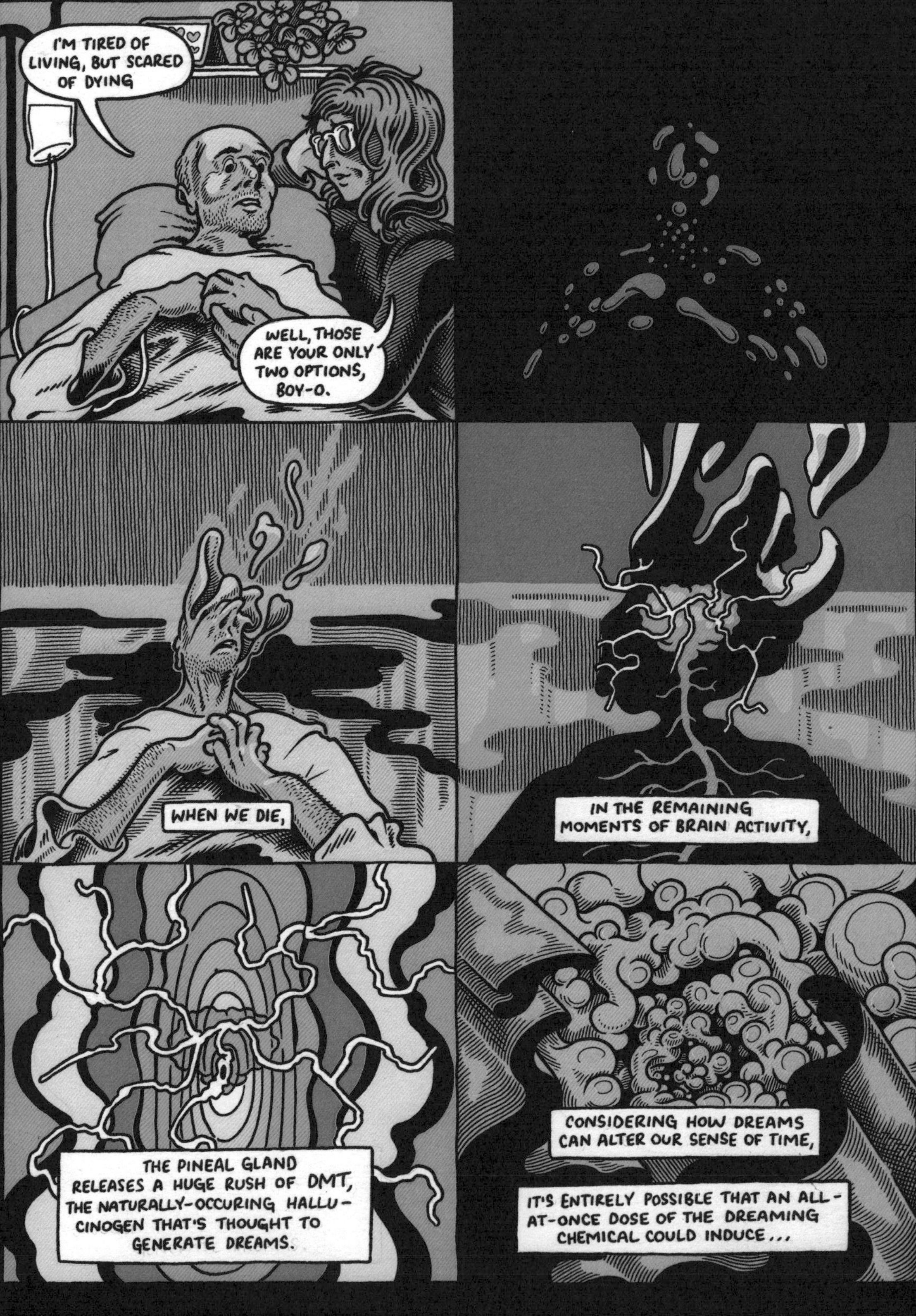
I'M TIRED OF LIVING, BUT SCARED OF DYING
WELL, THOSE ARE YOUR ONLY TWO OPTIONS, BOY-O.
WHEN WE DIE,
IN THE REMAINING MOMENTS OF BRAIN ACTIVITY,
THE PINEAL GLAND RELEASES A HUGE RUSH OF DMT, THE NATURALLY-OCCURING HALLU-CINOGEN THAT'S THOUGHT TO GENERATE DREAMS.
CONSIDERING HOW DREAMS CAN ALTER OUR SENSE OF TIME,
IT'S ENTIRELY POSSIBLE THAT AN ALL-AT-ONCE DOSE OF THE DREAMING CHEMICAL COULD INDUCE...

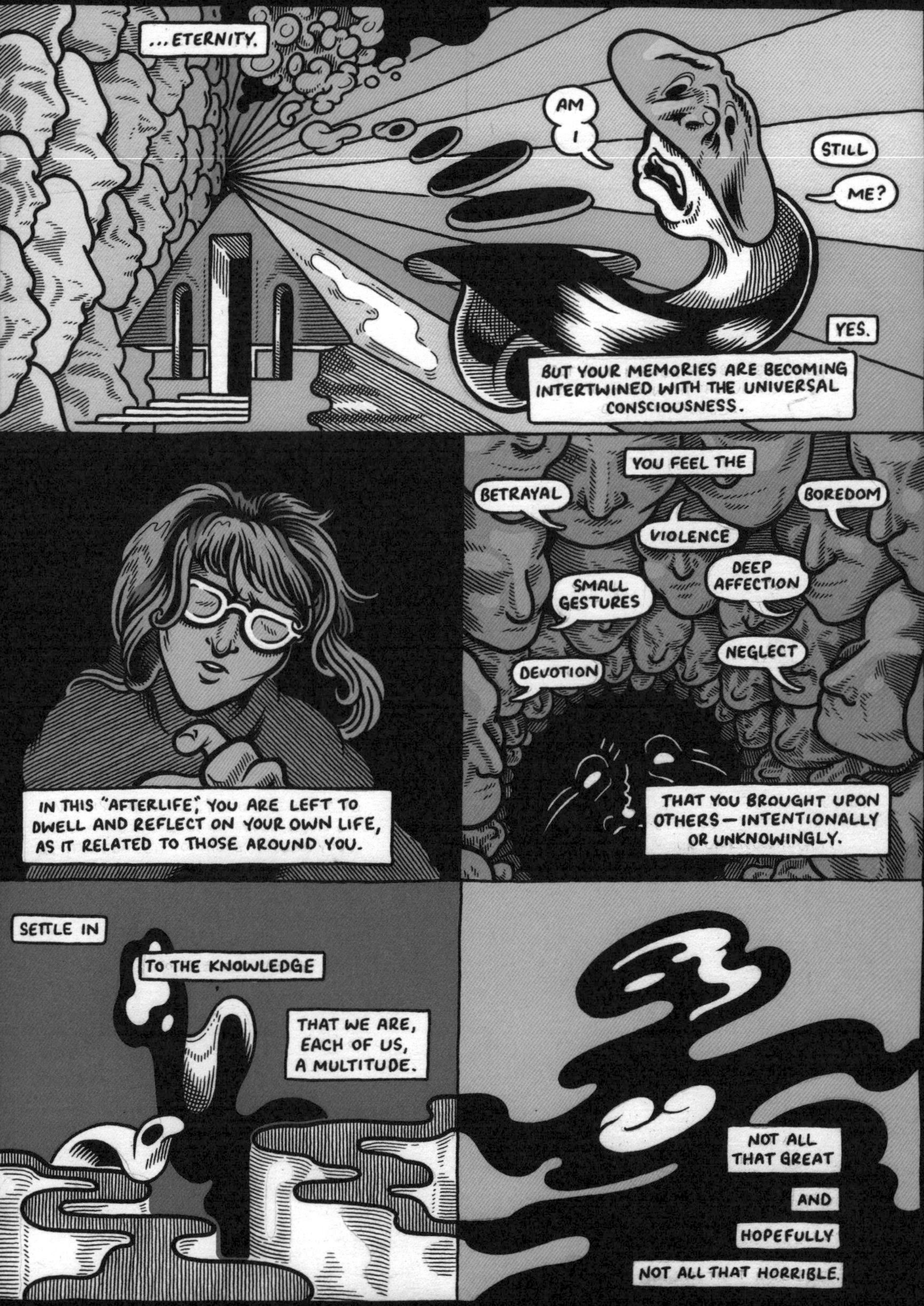
...ETERNITY.
AM I
STILL ME?
YES.
BUT YOUR MEMORIES ARE BECOMING INTERTWINED WITH THE UNIVERSAL CONSCIOUSNESS.
IN THIS "AFTERLIFE," YOU ARE LEFT TO DWELL AND REFLECT ON YOUR OWN LIFE, AS IT RELATED TO THOSE AROUND YOU.
YOU FEEL THE
BETRAYAL
BOREDOM
VIOLENCE
DEEP AFFECTION
SMALL GESTURES
NEGLECT
DEVOTION
THAT YOU BROUGHT UPON OTHERS—INTENTIONALLY OR UNKNOWINGLY.
SETTLE IN
TO THE KNOWLEDGE
THAT WE ARE, EACH OF US, A MULTITUDE.
NOT ALL THAT GREAT
AND
HOPEFULLY
NOT ALL THAT HORRIBLE.

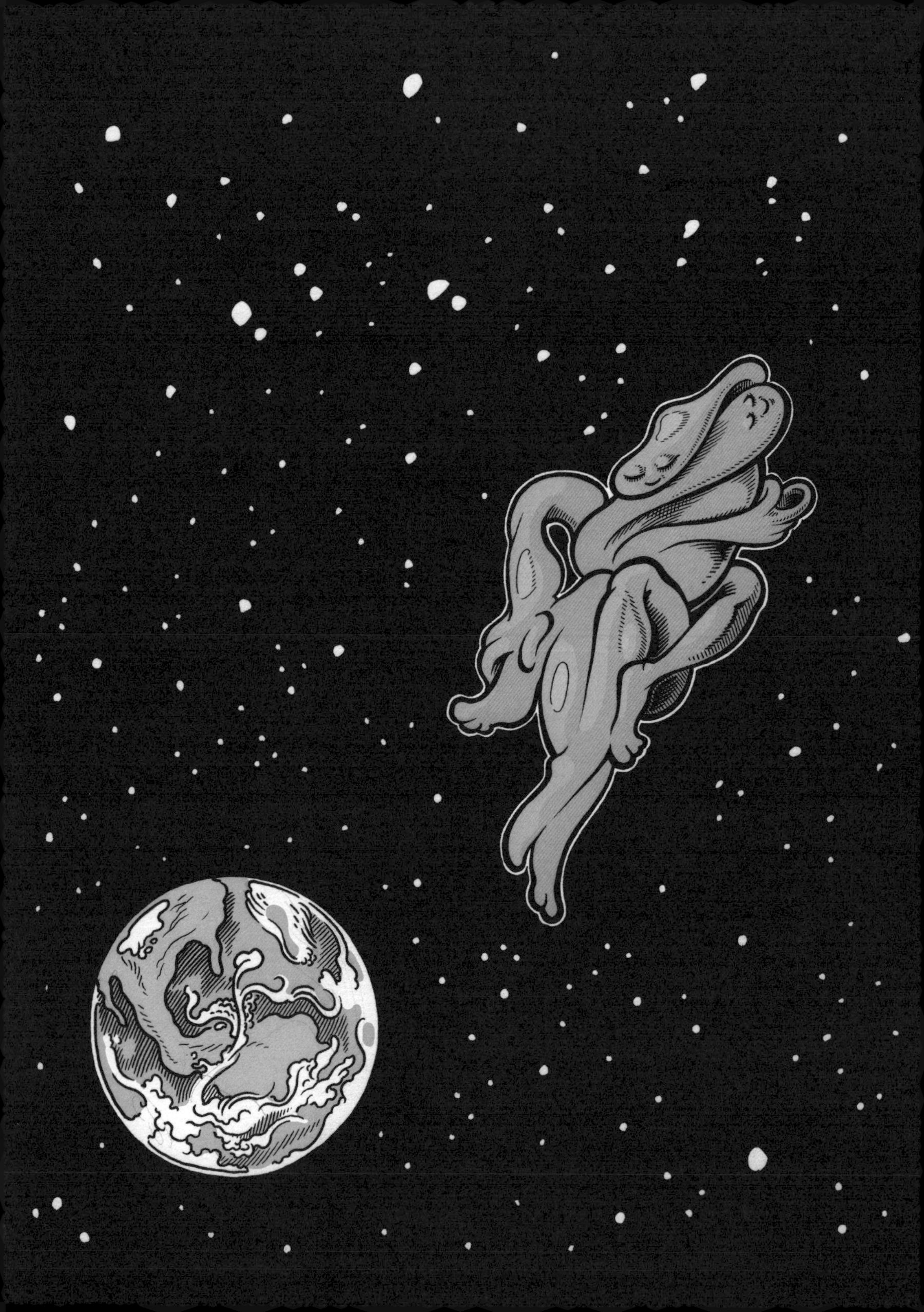

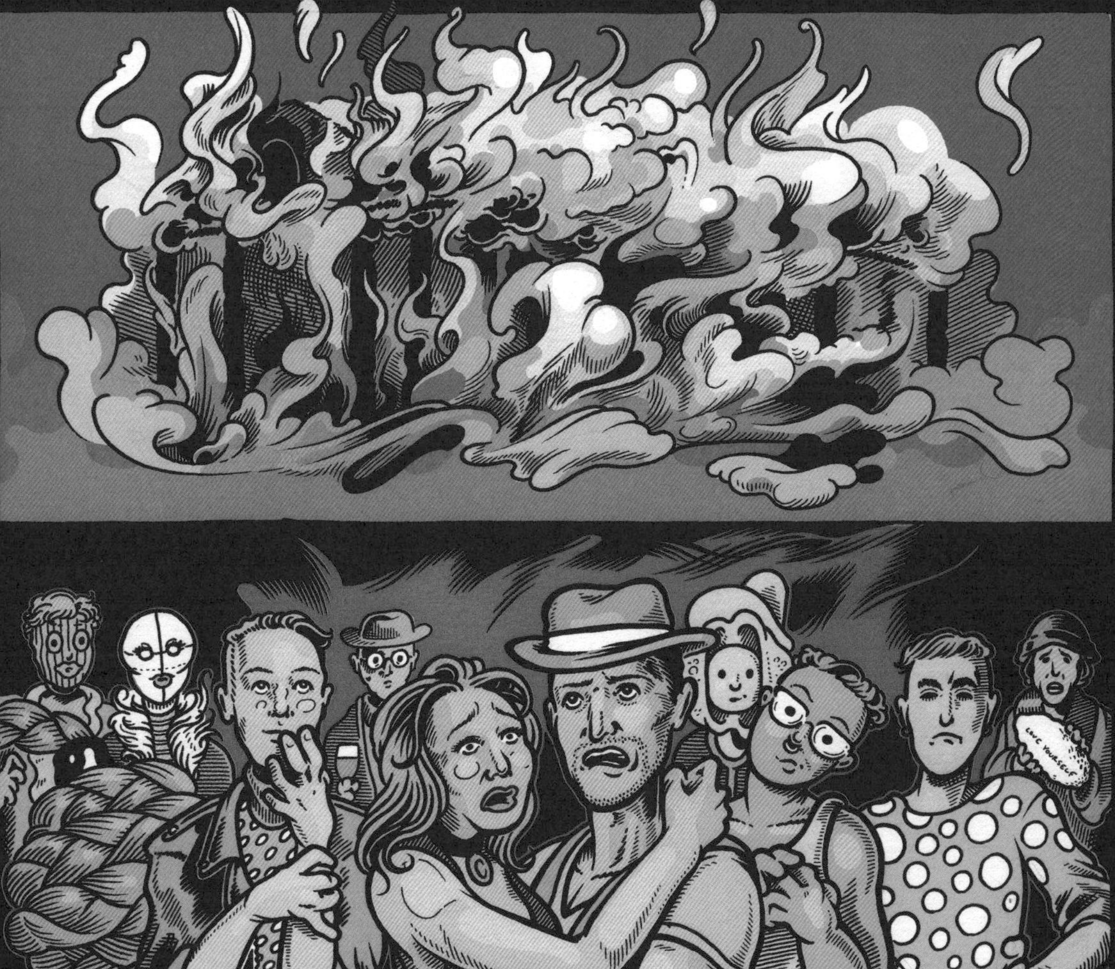
LOVE YOURSELF

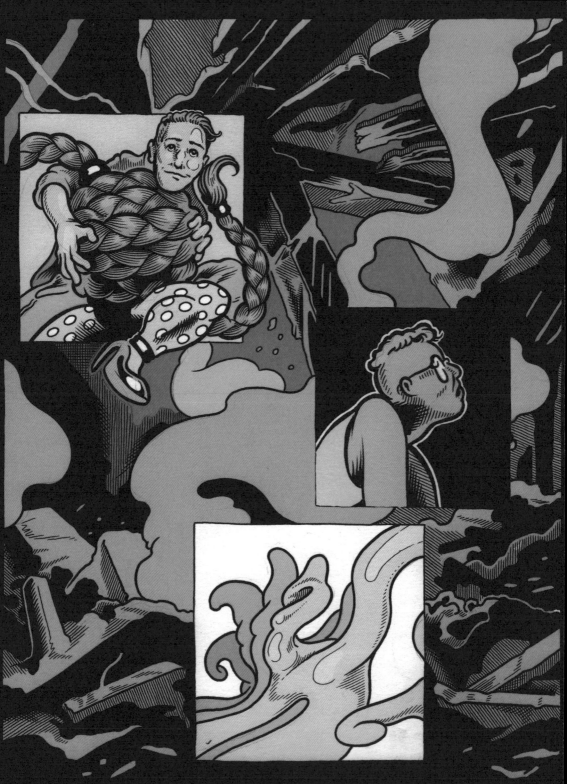

MAYBE YOU'RE CLOSER
TO HERE THAN YOU
IMAGINE.

AM I STILL TAKING MINUTES FOR THIS MEETING, OR...?

THANK YOU:

EKW

LIVES IN TORONTO, CANADA, MAKING COMICS + ILLUSTRATIONS. HIS WORK HAS BEEN NOMINATED FOR EISNER, LAMBDA, AND DOUG WRIGHT AWARDS. HE CONTRIBUTES COMIC CONCERT REVIEWS TO NOW MAGAZINE.

OTHER WORKS:
CONDO HEARTBREAK DISCO (KOYAMA PRESS); LEY LINES: HOW DOES IT FEEL IN MY ARMS? (CZAP BOOKS / GRINDSTONE COMICS); BABYBEL WAX BODYSUIT (RETROFIT / BIG PLANET); HUNGRY BOTTOM COMICS (COLOUR CODE)

TO KEITH COLE, FOR GENEROUSLY GRANTING ME PERMISSION TO ADAPT HIS 2013 SPEECH INTO THE VIDEOFAG COMIC. VIDEOFAG CLOSED ITS DOORS IN 2016. I'M GRATEFUL TO WILLIAM AND JORDAN FOR INVITING SO MANY OF US TO EXPRESS OURSELVES AND SHOW WORK IN THEIR SPACE (YEP, THEIR SPACE! THEY LIVED IN THE BACK OF VIDEOFAG!) FOR MORE INFO, CHECK OUT THE VIDEOFAG BOOK, AVAILABLE FOR ORDER ON BOOKTHUG.CA IN THE VIDEOFAG COMIC, I DEPICTED WORK FROM HANNAH ENKEL & PHILIP SHELTON ("LONG LIVE THE WORKING CLASS"), JESS DOBKIN, AND LIDO PIMIENTA. CHECK OUT THEIR STUFF!!

SEVERAL OF THESE STORIES ORIGINALLY APPEARED ON OMG! BLOG BIG THANKS TO FRANK GRIGGS FOR OFFERING ME THAT OPPORTUNITY. THANKS ALSO TO THE PRISM COMICS PEEPS FOR AWARDING ME THE 2018 QUEER PRESS GRANT. IT HELPED BIG TIME IN THE COMPLETION AND PROMOTION OF THIS BOOK.

THANKS TO JARED SMITH + BOX BROWN, JUSTIN HALL, FIONA SMYTH, GB JONES, SAM BOWMAN, MAURICE VELLEKOOP, MAGGIE MACDONALD, VESNA ASANOVIC, ANNE KOYAMA, KIM JOOHA, ROB KIRBY, LEINEY CHIANG, COMEAU, THE BEGUILING, MY FOLKS,

AND, MOST OF ALL, TO ALON FREEMAN, FOR HIS SUPPORT AND PATIENCE. I LOVE YOU, MONSIEUR!

THIS BOOK IS DEDICATED TO THE TORONTO OVERDOSE PREVENTION SOCIETY, PARKDALE ORGANIZED, QUEERS CRASH THE BEAT, AND ANYONE OUT THERE DOING BRAVE WORK, WITH COMPASSION AND JUSTICE IN THEIR HEARTS.